DID EVERYONE HAVE
AN IMAGINARY FRIEND
(OR JUST ME)?

DID EVERYONE HAVE AN IMAGINARY FRIEND (OR JUST ME?)

ADVENTURES IN BOYHOOD

JAY ELLIS

ONE WORLD
NEW YORK

Did Everyone Have an Imaginary Friend (or Just Me)?
is a work of nonfiction. Some names and
identifying details have been changed.

Published in the United States by One World,
an imprint of Random House, a division of
Penguin Random House LLC, New York.

One World and colophon are registered trademarks of
Penguin Random House LLC.

LIBRARY OF CONGRESS CATALOGING-IN-PUBLICATION DATA
Names: Ellis, Jay, author.
Title: Did everyone have an imaginary friend or just me? / Jay Ellis.
Description: New York: One World, [2024]
Identifiers: LCCN 2023052282 (print) | LCCN 2023052283 (ebook) |
ISBN 9780593243190 (hardcover) | ISBN 9780593243206 (ebook)
Subjects: LCSH: Ellis, Jay, 1981- | Ellis, Jay, 1981—Childhood and
youth. | African American actors—Biography. | African American
children—Social conditions. | Imaginary companions. |
United States—Race relations—History—20th century.
Classification: LCC PN2287.E455 A3 2024 (print) |
LCC PN2287.E455 (ebook) | DDC 818/.603 [B]—dc23/eng/20240423
LC record available at https://lccn.loc.gov/2023052282
LC ebook record available at https://lccn.loc.gov/2023052283

Illustration on page 4 by Mel Cerri
All photographs are courtesy of the author

Printed in the United States of America on acid-free paper

oneworldlit.com

1 2 3 4 5 6 7 8 9

First Edition

Book design by Edwin A. Vazquez

To imagination . . .
To the village that helped raise me . . .
To my daughter, may your imagination run wild & free . . .
To friends, imaginary & not.

CONTENTS

DID EVERYONE HAVE AN IMAGINARY FRIEND (OR JUST ME)?

Friends,
How many of us have them?
Friends,
Ones we can depend on.
—WHODINI

Imagination
creates the situation,
and, then, the situation
creates imagination.
—JAMES BALDWIN

In a land where daydreams dance with glee,
Children's imagination runs wild and free.
With cardboard castles and spaceships of tin,
Endless adventures they'll steadfastly begin.

Hours float by in a world all their own,
From pirates to fairies, they make it known.
Oh, the delight when simplicity is spun!
Children's imagination—always number one.
—CATHERINE PULSIFER

MIKEY & ME: INTRO

"Oh hell naw! We ain't 'bout to be no croc's dinner!"

BEING A KID, ESPECIALLY A BLACK KID AND A BLACK BOY BACK in the day, was confusing, dangerous, fun, and alluring. There were so many mixed messages of how to be—what was cool, what was right, who to emulate, who to disavow. We were court-chasing hoop dreamers and Starter jacket–wearing block dwellers who debated and acted out iconic scenes from the greatest movies, television shows, and music videos ever made, all while staying, or trying to stay, alert to the presence of crack cocaine, gang violence, the ever-present threat of police violence, and an overzealous government that made overpopulating prisons with young Black men its mission. Every day there was a new threat to our safety, and every day the stakes felt higher than the day before. To be afraid and intrigued at once was ordinary.

I came of age in a wild time. I know every person in the history of the world has said that the era they grew up in was "iconic," but when you're an '80s baby who came of age in the '90s and you say it, it hits a little different:

Reaganomics. Inflation. *Hollywood Shuffle*. The War on ~~Drugs~~ People of Color. The rise of hip-hop. *Scarface*. Michael Jackson sleeping in a hyperbaric chamber with a pet monkey. Golden era of the NBA; Chicago Bulls. The first cellphone. *Do the Right Thing*. A *billion* people watched Prince Charles and Princess Diana get married. Crack cocaine. Prison population boom. *Coming to America*. Cabbage Patch dolls. Whitney Houston. *Top Gun*. CD players. HIV / AIDS. Twenty-four-hour news channels. *School Daze*. Eighty-three million people watched to see who shot J. R. Ewing. *Back to the Future*. Michael Jordan. "Can we talk . . . for a minute?" The rise of the Bloods and Crips. "Yo' momma" jokes. *Teenage Mutant Ninja Turtles*. *Harlem Nights*. The personal computer. Cleo the Psychic. MTV. The "Three Strikes" law. The Gulf War. *He Got Game*. "I did not have sexual relations with that woman." *The Real World*. Dial-up internet. "Heyyyyy Macarena, aight." Pagers. Tupac. Ninety-five million people watched the O. J. Simpson verdict. Sony PlayStation. Aaliyah. Ebonics. Cuban Adjustment Act. *Boyz N the Hood*. Tamagotchi Eggs. Tony Robbins. "It never rains in Southern California." *Juice*. *Seinfeld*. The Unabomber. The Notorious B.I.G. *The Fresh Prince of Bel-Air*. Rodney King. Hooked on Phonics. *Love & Basketball*. Clinton Crime Bill. Jay-Z. *Dead Presidents*.

1992 Dream Team. Matthew Shepard. *Martin.* The first gene therapy trial. Janet Jackson. NAFTA. *In Living Color.* Oklahoma City Bombing. *Toy Story.* Anita Hill. Crystal Pepsi. Oprah. *Forrest Gump.* Destiny's Child. Dr. Martens. *Living Single.* Jeffrey Dahmer. *Clueless.* "I got the hook up, holla if you hear me." Pogs. *Jurassic Park.* Lauryn Hill. *Fight Club.* Mariah Carey. FUBU. *Wu-Tang Forever.*

If young you was anything like young me, then you needed something to give you some semblance of control in a chaotic/uncontrollable world. That's how Mikey, my imaginary friend, came into my life.

Before we get started talking about imaginary stuff, I have to be real with you: For a long time I thought I was the kid, Haley Joel Osment, from *The Sixth Sense* and maybe, just maybe, there was the possibility I was seeing dead people. Or maybe I was the less dramatic version—Whoopi Goldberg in *Ghost.* Perhaps Mikey was my Patrick Swayze. When you're five—or any age—the last thing you want is to *feel* someone who isn't really there wrapping their arms around you while you're sitting at a pottery wheel. Nobody wants that superpower. As I got older, I realized I wasn't seeing dead people after all. But instead, I had an imaginary friend that felt more like an older brother. I decided I wanted to understand what an imaginary friend actually is. Was Mikey a past-life version of me? Did my soul split in two? Was this very stylish and charming person part of me? Or maybe it was a person from a parallel universe? A person I wanted to be? What exactly is an imaginary friend? And why did I have one?

At heart, I'm a student. I love to learn. I've taken classes or courses between every season of every show and every movie I've done over the last decade. Learning is my adult way of working through the inability to be able to control the uncontrollable. I might not be able to control something, but if I can learn about it, I have a better understanding and can find my own version of comfort. Finding out more about imaginary friends was no different, except there are no classes on childhood imaginary friends. But, as my nana would say, "It's on the Googles, ain't it?" Yes, Nana, your rhetorical question about the internet you barely know how to use is correct. I started digging around the internet, and according to developmental psychologist Marjorie Taylor (NOT to be confused with the "politician" from Georgia): "An imaginary companion is a friend whom a child has created, talks about, or interacts with on a regular basis."*

Mikey *was* a companion I created and interacted with. He was real to me. But of all the things in the world I could have picked—Transformers, He-Man, Inspector Gadget, Run-DMC, G.I. Joe, Another Bad Creation, Michael Jackson's pet monkey, Bruce Leeroy—of all of the possibilities, I chose a human-like imaginary friend.

> Over the course of nearly 30 years, Taylor has heard
> of imaginary friends who can fly, live on the moon,
> become invisible, and breathe fire, and who can take

---

* Source (so you can't say I imagined it): Eileen Kennedy-Moore, "Imaginary Friends: Are Invisible Friends a Sign of Social Problems?" *Psychology Today*, January 2013.

the form of aliens, reptiles, and even real objects like stuffed animals.*

Little boys' imaginary friends are frequently characters who are more competent than they are, such as superheroes or beings with powers, she says.†

I picked a fly young Black man who dressed in the latest and rocked the freshest haircut, which swept through every Black neighborhood from the Tri-State down to the DMV, across Southside Chicago, and out to South Central Los Angeles: the flattop. There was something reassuring about his easy demeanor, his curiosity, and his ability to calm my fears—all while hyping me up and guiding me through the treacherous years of young adulthood—that made him not only profoundly important, but necessary to me and for me.

SO HOW DID MIKEY ACTUALLY "COME TO BE"? WELL, GROWING UP as an only child, I was alone most of the time. It was hard to keep friends because my military family moved around a lot. At home I didn't have a bully older brother, like Wayne Arnold from *The Wonder Years,* or a know-it-all sister, like Vanessa Huxtable from *The Cosby Show,* to talk to, play with,

---

* Lauren J. Young, "The Truth About Imaginary Friends (Developmental Psychologist Marjorie Taylor Has Turned Our Understanding of Imaginary Companions Upside Down)," ScienceFriday.com, May 25, 2016.
  † Dave McGinn, "Hello, My (Imaginary) Friend," *Globe and Mail,* January 7, 2016.

learn from, or even blame things on when I got in trouble—like the time I found out my best friend and I were dating the same girl, which caused me to put a hole in the wall that I tried to cover with an Elmer's glue stick and leftover wallpaper I found in the garage.

So, like any other kid in the world with a myriad of conflicting messages being thrown at them daily, while also in pursuit of authentic friendship, I went on a search to find who would become my best friend for life, and by "search" I mean I created Mikey. And he was the shit!

Creating an imaginary friend wasn't my first choice, but my subconscious had to do something to "control" the overwhelming feeling—my heart beating fast, sounds beginning to warble, time creeping to a crawl—that occurred every time I had to walk into a new school and try to make new friends, and every time I had to leave the friends I did make, usually with no goodbyes or closure, knowing I'd have to start over again.

Mikey came to me at night during a bad storm that seemed like a never-ending monsoon, when I was around four, almost five, years old. The pops of lightning lit up the walls of my room, creating shadows that looked like monsters coming to eat me. The thunder was so powerful that with each *BOOM!* the windows rattled so viciously that I was convinced someone was trying to break in and kidnap me. Who wouldn't want to take this toothless wonder of joy and inventiveness?

Thanks to my corn syrup–fueled overactive imagination, my bed was surrounded by a swamp full of crocodiles, naturally preventing me from getting out of bed and running to my parents' room. So, in a moment of panic, fear, and snapping crocodile teeth, Mikey popped up behind me, peering over my shoulder, and said—I can still hear his first words, like it was just earlier today—"Oh hell naw! We ain't 'bout to be no croc's dinner!"

Looking down at me was a teenage-ish boy who wore jean overalls with one strap down and a red, green, and black striped T-shirt. His glasses had shades attached that flipped up, and he had a tall flattop—basically a combination of Dwayne Wayne from *A Different World* meets Will Smith from *The Fresh Prince of Bel-Air* that, if you squinted hard enough, kind of looked like an older version of me. Almost immediately, I felt relaxed instead of scared by his presence. He felt like someone I had known for all of my very short life. He pivoted and sat next to me until the thunder slowed and the lightning dimmed. He told jokes, made small quips, and commented on things around my room. He was fun, goofy, smart, smooth, and well dressed—I knew instantly that Mikey was the coolest guy on the planet.

I tested this theory by asking the tough questions and gauging his responses:

"Why are my parents arguing with each other?"

"They are having a very passionate discussion about money and what happens when you don't have enough because your dad used it to buy a TV out of some guy's trunk but it was actually just a box filled with bricks," Mikey quickly replied. He then looked at me and softly said, "Sometimes folks just get carried away when they get excited."

"Is that why my parents wrestle in bed after they yell?"

"Uh, yeah, because the mattress . . . is safe for aggressive wrestling maneuvers." My parents were in their early twenties. They "wrestled" a lot.

Mikey and I laughed all night as a reaction to what I now realize was our anxiety. We told jokes, made up stories, and worked through various scenarios. He was everything I wanted in an older brother and a friend, and from that moment on, we were best friends. Mikey was kind of a Renaissance man, even if he was stuck in the late '80s with a serious case of arrested development. Mikey stood by me through every moment imaginable. Elementary, middle, and high school—yes, I said high school. Just keep reading. You'll see what I mean! From my first day at a new school to my first "fight," to my first kiss, to me trying to make losing my virginity last more than three and a half minutes—I recited the presidents in order, how far do you think I got?—there was no end to the amount of hell we raised.

From the time I was seven years old until my grandfather passed, right after I turned fifteen, I went on road trips with my grandparents every summer. One year, during a pit stop on one of our road trips, I got sick eating mounds and mounds of pink cotton candy—that warm, sticky, fabric-like sugar that magically melted in my mouth—while I watched Mikey go on the Batman ride at Six Flags St. Louis. My grandpa, Booker, was not happy. The cotton candy was to make me feel better because I didn't meet most of the height requirements for a lot of the rides. In the words of Jack Nicholson's Joker, "Have you ever danced with the devil in the pale moonlight?" No, but I have danced with some cotton candy in broad daylight. Truthfully, I was afraid of roller coasters—and grateful to the gods that my growth spurt hadn't happened yet. Therefore, while I got sick eating mounds of cotton candy, Mikey decided to show me that riding roller coasters might be scary but if he could do it and overcome his fears, so could I. Mikey did this often, showed me things would be okay by doing them first. So I spent the day eating cotton candy and watching Mikey ride roller coasters to prove his point. To me, an only child, he was the closest thing I'd have to an older, guinea pig sibling. The next time the opportunity presented itself, I rode (read: *I puked*).

As I got older, I rarely talked about my imaginary friend. I just assumed, as an only child who was used to having no one to ask, that I was one of the few people who had one. Because *obviously* only *I* could have been going through that experience. And I wasn't about to expose my childhood crazy while I was on a date in college or butt-naked in the locker room after a game, exclaiming, "Game was crazy tonight! Quick question, did any of you guys have an imaginary friend growing up?"

I began to wonder: If people did have imaginary friends, were they weeklong friends, casually discarded for a new toy or hobby? Did their imaginary friends help them through fears, or were they just playmates? How *real* were their imaginary friends, compared to Mikey?

Imaginary friends are a common—and normal— manifestation for many kids across many stages of development. In fact, by age 7, 65 percent of children will have had an imaginary friend, according to a 2004 study. The prime time for having imaginary friends is from the ages of 3 to 11.[*]

[*] Allie Volpe, "Why Kids Invent Imaginary Friends," *The Atlantic,* July 30, 2019.

Mikey was in my life for almost eight years. That's a long time, and imaginary or not, no matter how extraordinarily unique or run-of-the-mill it was, it had an impact on my life. Mikey was pivotal for me during a growth and development time, when I was beginning to process the people and world around me. Mikey's friendship helped me during the quiet times and in times of reflection—my childhood life was shaped by that relationship.

In the beginning of the COVID pandemic, while we were all in lockdown—and with folks in my profession unable to work—I had some extra time on my hands. After reading a few books, listening to six or seven podcasts, trying a new hobby, downloading Duolingo, burning a bunch of homemade bread, and watching a thousand movies and shows, I found myself—like many of us—searching for something deeper. I started digging through childhood pictures and middle school and high school yearbooks. In one sitting, I watched myself transform from a baby to hitting puberty. It was shocking—I really looked the same! Even through the baby hair, the missing teeth, the acne and the braces—parts of me were consistently present. With each picture, I replayed so many moments I had completely forgotten: apartments, friends, birthday parties, and family reunions. It was like a rush of memories popping in and out of my head. I laughed. I got lost in thought. I reminisced on the simplicity of the earlier times. I thought about things I hadn't thought about in decades. There was photo evidence of childhood dreams, events, and choices I made, which in the moment seemed to be asking life-altering questions:

*Should I risk getting put on blast and talk to the girl in
third period? Should I shower naked after gym or leave my*

boxers on? If I shower in my boxers do I go commando for the rest of the school day? Should I go to the NBA? College? Can I be a rapper? Do I like Duke or North Carolina? The 49ers or the Cowboys?

Life's crippling decisions, right? But then there were other choices and situations that felt so familiar, so a part of "everyday life" that I made them with ease. These were the decisions that shouldn't have been effortless, let alone normal and routine, and I didn't realize at the time how profound their impact would be on my growth:

Should I hug the block? Did I ruin my teenage parents' life? If I don't go to college does that mean I'll never get a job? Can I even get into college? Wait, are my white friends' parents racist? Does that mean my white friends are racist? Should I tell my parents I got pulled over again? Should I tell them I was scared? Is the cop going to use his gun on me? What exactly are Bloods and Crips? Should I be one? What if I'm not good at it? Will they jump me in and then jump me out? Will I survive? Is it Ku Klux Klan rally weekend downtown again? Nobody's gonna have a gun at the party tonight, right? If I get hit by a bullet at that party tonight, what was the last thing I said to my parents?

Figuring out how to move through various predicaments, how to ask questions and make decisions, is essentially what "growing up" entails, and for me, the consistent presence through all of it was Mikey. His presence in any given moment, a reminder of something he said, or a lesson I learned before he left accompanied me through all of the tribulations of my youth. Adventure after adventure; story after story; from childhood to young adulthood.

So, one day, after a few hours going down Imaginary Lane, and without giving it a second thought, I told a story about my imaginary friend on Instagram. On a late spring day, after being locked in the house for months, terrified I was going to run out of toilet paper and/or get this life-threatening virus if I didn't wipe down every single thing that came into the house—I recorded a short story, and before I could even lift my finger off the POST button, I began to sweat. I was already questioning, *Why in the HELL did I post that?* I'm not Kevin Hart telling his *Straight from the Hart* stories in a bathrobe with a glass of two-billion-dollar wine. There was no way a story "about my imaginary friend" was going to be remotely entertaining or yield the same response as Dwayne Johnson or Oprah posting some overwhelmingly positive and motivating message. What did I expect? The gossip magazines were going to eat this up, the headline on *Page Six* will say, "JAY ELLIS HAVING A BREAKDOWN." Trevor Noah was definitely going to do a whole segment of *The Daily Show* chronicling how my best friend was imaginary. TMZ would be outside my house reporting from their tour bus in minutes. *Star* magazine and the *National Enquirer* are going to say I've been brainwashed by aliens. Everybody is going to have something to say when they see it, and Mikey will become a pariah. The media would try to tarnish or diminish one of the constants in my childhood life, a figure of safety, creativity, and endless childhood adventures—why did I put myself, or Mikey, in that position? I could hear the internet cackling:

*Aye, Jay out here on instagram talking 'bout imaginary
friends, he cracking y'all.*

Ahh, I knew his ass was crazy! Told y'all from the jump.

*These actors out here breaking down. Go look at Lawrence
IG. He need to shave.*

Typically, when I post something, I walk away from it. It's
out there and it's not mine anymore, the internet owns it. I
don't look to see the response—at least not for validation (because I know the internet is not where I'm going to get that
from!). However, after my post about Mikey, I was refreshing
my feed every seven seconds to read comments. I was out—
REFRESH—feeling vulnerable; butt-naked with a four-month
overgrown beard—REFRESH—feeling like I'd let people in
on my childhood secret and that would end me. And within
seconds—REFRESH—the comments started loading in.

Over the first few days I got thousands of comments from
people telling me stories about their own imaginary friends
or their siblings' imaginary friends—or how they always
wanted an imaginary friend. So, Dr. Taylor was right, I wasn't
the only one. However, I realized that what Taylor did not
mention in her report is that while people do have imaginary
friends, they just don't talk about them. I can only assume
this is because of the same reasons I didn't: the fear or self-
consciousness that this imaginary co-conspirator, who helped
me navigate an uncontrollable and often unsafe world, was
something to feel shame about, rather than pride and grati-
tude. Or maybe they just put it behind them and forgot.

———

I HAVE A THEORY THAT THE MOST CREATIVE PEOPLE ON THE planet probably all had imaginary friends growing up. Some of your favorite singers, rappers, actors, comedians, and entertainers have made careers out of their curious minds, but what if, and this is a humble/unbiased/non-leading-off-the-top-of-the-dome question, what if these people have managed to morph their imaginary friends into "alter egos" or "personas"? What if we never "lose" our imaginary friends, but instead repurpose them to serve us in other ways? So, once again, I listened to Nana and went on the Googles to see if anyone else out there had the same hypothesis.

> "Take all the most creative people you know," says Jonathan Plucker, a creativity researcher at the University of Connecticut who is researching how people, especially students, communicate their creativity to others. "It doesn't matter if they are artists or engineers or entrepreneurs. Now look for common denominators among them. What you are most likely to find if you do some digging is that they had an imaginary friend in childhood."*

Beyoncé blessed the world with a whole album inspired by her alter ego, Sasha Fierce, and the first track on Jay-Z's *4:44* album is titled "Kill Jay Z." He spends two minutes and

---

* Dave McGinn, "Hello, My (Imaginary) Friend," *Globe and Mail,* January 7, 2016.

fifty-eight seconds on a No I.D.–produced track killing his own persona and ego to give way to a new understanding and perspective. Kobe became Mamba! And still is. Can you imagine Lady Gaga's imaginary friend? She wore raw meat as a dress! Or Bowie's Ziggy Stardust! Also, Jay & Bey forever.

We all have created a persona for ourselves, whether we realize it or not, and the more you live in a public space (the internet counts!) where you are exposed to hundreds, thousands, or millions of people a day, the more likely you are to have built a persona to protect yourself or what's sacred to you. If you're aware of it, it's healthy. It's smart. Doesn't matter what field you're in, it's hard to sustain day after day if you give everything every day. Your persona helps you recharge yourself, it helps you keep something for yourself. Without that help, you burn out. You feel used and unappreciated. Or, even worse, you have nothing to give, but can't stop. You give faster than you can replenish. It's inevitable. Your magic is yours and yes, you can and even should share it with people, but that doesn't mean you have to give it all away. You have to find a way to protect what fuels you, inspires you, and makes you happy. This is what having a developed persona has done in my life: protected what's sacred.

Imaginary friends help kids protect, nurture, and explore their joy, wonder, and magic. Kids don't need to understand how to navigate the expectations of others; they don't need a "public face," as adults do. As kids, we are less self-conscious and less calculated; we're more unencumbered and free. And that space, between self-conscious and free, is where an imaginary friend comes in. Perhaps an imaginary friend is created or manifested to help kids understand the world in relation to themselves—their burgeoning desires, curiosities, joys, traumas, questions. Or maybe they show up to help allow for freedom, help create space for them. By a friend's very imagined existence and presence in their lives, kids are keeping their sense of play and wonder engaged. Their curiosity about the world is nurtured and encouraged, and, most importantly, protected.

Mikey helped me feel safe in questioning why the world was the way it was, and in imagining how the world, and my life, could be. While imaginary friends and personas are two different concepts, and happen at different stages in one's life, in their most basic function they are the same; both are created to safeguard and preserve.

When I was eight or nine years old, Mikey and I, inspired by Doc Brown and Marty McFly and wanting to know how our future would turn out, tried to go "back to the future" by building a time machine out of an old engine we found in an abandoned garage in the officers' housing area on the base we lived on. Once we started building, we realized we couldn't travel to the future because there was a shortage of "flux capacitors" in my neighborhood. For two days, we searched the neighborhood looking for engines we could use as a portal—Mikey told me to—and despite the curious, confused, or worried glances we got, we persisted until we found one in the storage shed of a garage that was so dust- and cobweb-filled it looked like it had been abandoned years before. Mikey nurtured my spirit of exploration while I was trying to figure out what my life would or could be.

As an only child who went to twelve schools in thirteen years because of my dad's Air Force career, I rarely got the chance to make long-term, deep friendships. On average I changed schools once a year. I was also a very curious, and slightly mischievous, kid. Before Mikey, I adventured alone, tested hypotheses, and occasionally—or often, depending on who you asked—pushed the limits. Maybe I created Mikey to have someone to blame for all the trouble *he* got us into. Listen, nobody in my family spared the rod. And I couldn't get *all* the whoopings. Was Mikey just a scapegoat? Or perhaps Mikey's presence was some kind of coping mechanism to help me deal with moving around and entering new environments over and over. It's hard to say the exact reason for his formation, but having him enter my life allowed me a safe space to explore. There are so many experiences I ultimately learned and grew from because of Mikey. He pushed me, and when I doubted myself or wasn't sure what to do, he gave me guidance.

We spent days frustratingly trying to get the engine to turn into a proper time machine. I felt I needed to know what was going to happen. I was fixated. Mikey patiently helped me let go by coaxing me into playing basketball, helping my mom cook, and exploring our neighborhood. This was my first lesson in being present and not obsessed with the future; in giving up control. Trying to rush the steps of life and get to the future meant that I would lose the moment I was in, and all that the moment could offer me. In this case, it was my childhood.

As I got older and more confident, and became less dependent on Mikey, he began to show his face less. This was around the time I entered into my "I'm the man" phase and started walking through the hall of my parents' house and my school with my chest puffed out. Mikey transitioned from someone I could clearly see to a guiding voice in my head. It seemed Mikey taught me everything he knew, and he was leaving me on my own to face this new colorful, wonderfully depressing, yet exciting world called middle school . . . also known as one of the cruelest places on earth.

I felt ready for the world, like I could take on anything and navigate any situation because of all we had been through together. Mikey's guidance helped me figure out how to get better at hiding things from my parents; log into AOL chat rooms and make up different identities; skip school by having a friend call the attendance office pretending to be my mom; talk my history teacher into letting me go to the gym during class to work on my free throws for the "honor of the school"; and talk to the ladies.

In all seriousness, before Mikey left, he did give me a few jewels of wisdom that I have never forgotten and that I still carry with me:

- Trust my instincts
- Always remember to find ways to play or have fun
- Say "Hi" or "What up?" or "What's good?" first when I enter a room
- Feel comfortable with who I am, no matter the situation; Do you!

As I pushed through my late teens, the voice in my head became the voice formerly known as Mikey and instead revealed itself as my subconscious. I was older, reading more, and as my Big Ma would say, I was learn'ed. At that point, I knew too much to still believe my imaginary friend was ever anything more than a figment of my imagination. Looking

back now, even during the post-Mikey years, my consciousness was helping me navigate through the muddy waters of
my chronically disrupted childhood, my acne-ridden adoles-
cence, and braces-faced coming-of-age years. That voice, *my*
voice, was a crutch that helped me cope with all the things I
couldn't talk to a sibling, a parent, or anyone else about; all
the things I wanted and felt I needed to understand.

I may have started to understand that the voice belonged
to me and not Mikey, and therefore I began to consult Mikey
less on a day-to-day basis, but there were still moments when
I needed to be hyped-up in order to get through challenging
situations. Like playing full-court one-on-one with the best
player on my high school's team, Ryan Humphrey. Ryan was
dubbed "Skywalker" by Dick Vitale because he had a 46-inch
vertical. After his college career he went on to play in the
NBA. I needed the hype and care that day in the field house at
Booker T. Washington High School when Ryan flew through
the air like Superman and dunked on me . . . repeatedly! The
voice kept me going, grinding, and I was a better player for it.

That same voice kept me from kicking it with the Three
Dre's. The Three Dre's got their moniker because they were
each named Andre. And the universal hood nickname for
Andre is "Dre." Popularized because the most infamous, successful, and popular "Dre" ever known to man also had the
very special distinction of being a doctor: Dr. Dre. Individually, the Three Dre's were three great guys, gifted athletes and
hood-smart, too . . . well, except one. But when the three of
them got together, there was smoke in the city—literally because they smoked hella weed, and metaphorically because
they always caused trouble that usually led to more trouble.
Like the time they found our tenth-grade English teacher's

car keys and tried to get me to go with them on a joyride. Or the time they nearly talked me into smoking weed for the first time but instead Imani volunteered before me. She had an allergic reaction causing her throat and face to swell up like Will Smith in *Hitch*, and in all of the panic she had to be rushed to the hospital. Bullet dodged thanks to that voice in my head that said, *Are you tripping? The Three Dre's together? You don't have time to get killed when you get home. It's not in the plan.*

By the time I moved off to college there was nothing that was remotely related to Mikey in my life. Like many others, I was non-actively listening to my subconscious. I paid no mind to my thought process.

In 2017, researchers at University College London described these five purposes for having an imaginary friend:

1. problem-solving and emotion management
2. exploring ideals
3. having a companion for fantasy play
4. having someone to overcome loneliness
5. allowing children to explore behaviors and roles in relationships*

Mikey was all of those scientifically studied and hypothesized things and much more to me. He was a friend, a big

* Karen Majors and Ed Baines, "Children's Play with Their Imaginary Companions: Parent Experiences and Perceptions of the Characteristics of the Imaginary Companions and Purposes Served," *Educational and Child Psychology* 34 (3): 37–56.

brother, a sounding board, an extra pair of eyes and ears, a fall guy, a proxy for feelings I didn't know how to voice, a style icon, my Cyrano de Bergerac, and a few times a lifesaver, literally. Now that I've had time and separation from Mikey, I have a whole new perspective and appreciation for all the things we went through together, and all the lessons I learned that still apply to my life as an adult. And although my parents, grandparents, and most people around me couldn't stand my incessant talking about Mikey and insistence that there be room for him at the dinner table, without them letting my imagination run wild, my life at many turns could have gone a very different way.

I'm sure many Black parents would have had me prayed over and bathed in anointing oil—I had an abnormal amount of anointing oil on my forehead growing up, but for different reasons—or told me to sit down, be quiet, and quit it. But without the support of my family, whether because they found it entertaining, encouraging, or lacked the patience to deal with it, I wouldn't be who I am today. If my imagination hadn't been allowed to do its thing, I wouldn't have had the stories and memories that led me to the burning question that started this book's journey: Why did I have an imaginary friend?

This ain't a memoir. I haven't lived enough life for that. This is a book filled with vignettes of childhood. This is about a very specific moment in time—in both my life and the world I inhabited—and how that moment influenced or made room for my imagination to run wild. The stories in this book are about growing up with an overactive imagination in a paradoxical society that forces kids into the asinine and hella boring existence of "fitting in" or being "normal" while inundating them with messages of inferiority, hyper-sexualization, violence, fear, prison, and consumerism. Coming of age and trying to fit in and stand out at the same time. The stories in this book are about a young Black boy who grew up where a normal night could result in an outburst of violence followed by watching "picture perfect" suburban teenage films about love. All of these stories, moments, and reflections were a journey through self-discovery. And as confusing and conflicting as the journey was, I had Mikey by my side to help me get through it all.

Now, let me tell you a bunch of embarrassing, ridiculous, and heartbreaking stories about how my childhood imaginary friend shaped my life.

ACT A FOOL WIT' IT

"Yo donna South Carolina."

FOR A STRETCH, MIKEY WAS A BIG CONCERN FOR MY YOUNG parents. It started out innocent enough—I was an only child with a colorful imagination, and then one day I came in talking about Mikey, my imaginary friend. Based on the fact that we had literally caused a small sandstorm and ruined someone's wedding, it was clear that if left to our own devices for long enough, we probably would have decimated entire city blocks of whichever random city we were living in at that time.

> *Dear bride, whose wedding Mikey made me ruin, if you are reading this and still married to that square in the ill-fitting tux, I apologize for ruining what was supposed to be the best day of your life . . . but those seagulls on the beach had it coming. They were taunting me all day with their stupid, squawking laugh and Mikey said the best way to shut them up was to teach them a lesson. They had to*

learn. By throwing sand bombs, seashells, and beach trash at those cackling seagulls. Your dress was an unfortunate casualty of war.

While communicating with each other through telepathy and the sides of their eyes, my parents decided to question me. "Sit down right here," my dad said. They interrogated me for about twenty minutes about Mikey's location in the house, what he looked like, when he came around, and what—if anything—he was telling me to do. They needed to know he wasn't a grown man sneaking into our house. They didn't seem convinced by my explanations, but after a few nights of sleeping with one eye open, they realized Mikey wasn't a ghost or a man crawling into the house through a hidden passage. They not only tolerated me having an imaginary friend, after a while my mom was even encouraging. One year, she baked two cakes for my birthday. She thought we had the same birthday, we didn't, I was pissed. If you're an only, you get me.

I LIKE TO THINK OF MY CHILDHOOD YEARS AS "BEHAVIORALLY challenged." The popular lore I stick to is that Mikey got me into a lot of trouble, but the years before Mikey were filled with plenty of transgressions. When I was three years old, my mom got a call that she needed to come pick me up from preschool. When she arrived, the teacher informed her that I had bitten three kids since the school day started. Even after being separated from other kids, I would find someone to sink my cannibal teeth into the moment I was released back to gen pop. This had been going on for weeks. And it seemed the situation was getting worse. They couldn't control me and I had bitten so many of the kids that pretty much all of them were scared to play with me. Apex predator or not, the teacher told my mom that she needed to find a new school to take me to because I was no longer welcome at Small World.

My mom and dad began to trade days off with their co-workers like kids trading Ken Griffey Jr. and Bo Jackson baseball cards, in order to be home with me until they could find a new daycare to send me to. It wasn't until months later that I was enrolled at Little Stinkers.

The daycare operated out of the owner's home. She had added an addition to the back of her ranch-style house, which is where us kids spent most of our time. And on Fridays she always brought an outside activity to the daycare. Like a petting zoo where we rode ponies (see the pic of me on a pony with a cowboy hat from the previous chapter). I had been at Little Stinkers incident-free for about four or five months when one day I woke up and chose to upend all the hard work and self-control my four-year-old self had put in; I chose violence.

Just before our afternoon nap, my mom got a call at work again. One embarrassing conversation with her boss and two bus rides later, she showed up to find me sitting in a corner by the front door, bags packed.

Before my mom could ask what had happened, my teacher sang like a falsetto in the Mississippi Mass Choir.

"Ms. Ellis—"

"*Mrs. Bryant*-Ellis," my mom corrected her.

The teacher narrowed her eyes. "Mrs. Bryant-Ellis, your son has expressed a colorful use of his vocabulary today by dropping several f-bombs even after I had spoken to him and asked him not to." My mom looked at me, expressionless like a cold-blooded killer.

"He what?" she said.

"He repeatedly used the f-word throughout the day within multiple contexts. He yelled it when another student dropped paint during craft time, he said it when he sat on the toilet after breakfast, and when I told him for the second time that we don't use that language here, he said, 'Eff you.' Mrs. Ellis—Byrant-Ellis—I'm not sure what you allow in your home, but I will not tolerate that behavior in mine." With that, she handed my mom my bag and showed her the door.

I was basically the four-year-old Samuel L. Jackson of Little Stinkers Daycare—a badge of honor I still carry to this day.

Daycare had become a place of chaos and confusion, of learning how to exist in the world with others, of no longer being the "only one." I spent most of my childhood until my tween years acting out to maintain my sense of control, of centerdom. I wanted attention. More specifically, my parents' attention. They were young. They had lives. They partied. They worked a lot. They were exhausted from working. They were trying to figure out how to make a marriage work. I thought doing crazy shit would get my parents to be home more. And if I couldn't get their attention, I was going to get somebody's.

WHEN MIKEY ENTERED, MY GOAL MAY HAVE BEEN THE SAME, BUT it was a lot more fun doing it with a partner in crime. It also took my antics up a notch (like the time I tried to fly a plane).

There was a period of time, from six to eight, where they tried everything to get me to drop Mikey: bribes, whoopings, groundings, as well as baseball, karate, and football. They even threatened me with Christmas gifts—explaining that if I didn't start "acting right," Santa wouldn't bring me anything. But none of it worked. I was loyal to a fault—still am—and Mikey was my ride or die.

Oddly enough, I gave up on believing in Santa Claus way before I gave up on believing in Mikey. I shanked Ol' Saint Nick in the back so quickly he didn't even get to turn around and see that I dealt the lethal blow with a sharpened candy cane. Although, this wasn't by choice. My dad was over giving credit to a jolly ol' white dude who lived in the coldest place on the planet, removed from the people he supposedly served, so he sat me down when I was around seven years old and told me his truth:

"Aye man, look. I can't keep giving credit to another man for all the work I do around here." My eyes opened wider than Bernie Mac's.

"Huh?" My dad's eyes pierced into mine.

"What I'm saying is, me and your mom are Santa Claus."

As soon as he said this, without skipping a beat, Mikey and I agreed that what he was trying to say was that my parents were actually Mr. and Mrs. Claus. They must have been waiting until I fell asleep to get in my dad's maroon Mazda RX-7 to fly to the North Pole, where they would work until the early hours of the morning until it was time for me to wake up. Why else hadn't they gotten rid of the heavy coats in the closet? We were living in the South! Mikey, who at this point was unable to contain himself because he finally knew the truth behind one of the greatest mythologies of all time, whispered into my ear, "Ask them to take you with them to the North Pole."

"Can I go to the North Pole with you?" I asked my dad.

"North what? No. There is no North Pole . . . There is, but . . . Dammit. I wasn't saying . . . I was saying Santa Claus doesn't exist. Paula, talk to your son."

"Baby, what your father is saying is that Santa Claus isn't real," my mom said slowly. "We buy you all those gifts and put them under the tree."

Mikey and I stood there with blank stares, until Mikey pushed me along. I left the room and crawled into my Batman sheets, shutting the door and listening to Mikey spin down a Christmas miracle conspiracy theory hole. "This is the greatest cover-up in history! Your parents are Santa and Santa's wife, man! They had to try and tell you it wasn't real because they have to keep the secret." Slowly, I started to feel better, and that night we devised a plan to catch them in the act. We were certain that they were lying to us, covering up the fact that they worked with elves, gave gifts to every kid in the world, and that my dad grew and wore a beard down to his knees. Our plan was to stay up late, sneak into the trunk of my dad's Mazda, and ride with them to the North Pole.

On the first night, we crawled out my bedroom window facing the street and stood at the back of my dad's car waiting. The moon was so bright it lit up everything in a pale glow. Mikey and I waited and waited but my parents never showed up. Mikey had to pee, so we crawled back through the window and didn't come back out. We never did catch my parents, but we did learn that it was easier than we expected to sneak out. We also learned that f-bombs get the point across, but they didn't get us the exact attention we were looking for.

—

AFTER A WHILE, I COULDN'T KEEP BLAMING MY IMAGINARY FRIEND for the trouble I caused. When I was about eight years old, my parents had had enough. It all started with yet another phone call telling them they needed to come pick me up from an after-school program at the Bergstrom Air Force Base youth center. This time it was my dad who came—and he came in HOT. I was terrified. My action-figure-built dad stormed in, giant arms swinging by his side, his stride long and fierce. As soon as he reached Ms. Carol, the youth center director, she went off on him about how I was a bad kid and he wasn't doing a good job raising a young man. After they went back and forth about who's telling who how to raise a child, she told my dad I destroyed her car and he needed to pay to get it fixed. I had thrown rocks at a car that I didn't know was hers, and one of those rocks hit her car window in the exact right place, with just enough force to crack it. I tried to explain to my parents that Mikey was to blame, that he told me to do it, but they weren't trying to hear. "What'd he do? Throw an imaginary rock that broke the window? No!" my mom yelled, exasperated.

Ms. Carol kicked me out of the youth center on at least five or six other occasions. A few of those times were warranted, but most weren't. If we played Bloody Mary by locking a kid in the bathroom, Ms. Carol would kick us out. If we practiced our karate in the rec room and accidentally round-housed an innocent bystander, Ms. Carol would kick us out. If we started a friendly paint fight during arts and crafts day, Ms. Carol would kick us out. Ms. Carol's number-one tool for maintaining dominance and order over a bunch of elementary school kids was threatening to kick you out of the only place you could play safely with other kids without the fear of being out in the streets where you could get into real trouble.

I couldn't stand it. Mikey and I decided to show Ms. Carol what happens when a kid is kicked out of the youth center for a day, and how a single day can lead that kid to irrational behavior and hard life choices. So, we rocked her car.

Okay, it might not have been the most rational lesson, but Mikey and I were frustrated. Ms. Carol was constantly dangling her power over us, and I spent so much time feeling trapped and boxed in, rather than free and creative. I was too young to rationalize feeling trapped rather than feeling free to understand the situation for what it was, in order to work within it.

My parents had tried on numerous occasions to get ahold of the situation:

"This been going too damn long. You too old for all this. There's no such thing as imaginary friends. Now cut the bullshit!" my dad would yell.

"Mikey told me you'd say that."

The "talking-to" that I often got from my dad was usually accompanied with a belt and a week spent in my room grounded, writing the sentence *I'm too old for an imaginary friend*. It felt like I was committing sacrilege with every stroke of my blue Bic pen, but unfortunately for my parents, even with my backside and my right hand exhausted, I never abandoned Mikey and he never abandoned me.

—

AT TIMES, MIKEY WAS LIKE DEEBO IN THE ICE CUBE AND CHRIS Tucker classic *Friday*. He'd tell me what to do, take the gold chain my momma gave me, and then punk me for my bike so he could escape before I caught the back of a belt for doing something he told me to do! One would think I'd have had the upper hand with the imaginary friend *I* created, but it was quite the opposite. Evidenced by: "Children sometimes act subordinate to their creations, and their imaginary friends can cause kids to say and do things that would get them into trouble."*

Mikey liked to test the bounds a little too often. Like every young kid who loved basketball, because it was pumped into hyper-consumerism in the late '80s and early '90s—"I wanna be, I wanna be, I wanna be like Mike"—I wanted a pair of Jordans. That year, it was the Jordan 5s. They were "da bomb." White and red. Fat tongue. The number 23 hanging out in the back corner just to remind everyone they were Michael Jordan's shoes. They were also way too expensive for my father's non-officer Air Force check (he was in the reserves, and spent a weekend a month serving) and my mom's checks from two part-time jobs (while paying to go to college at

---

* Carl Gustav Jung, *The Collected Works of C. G. Jung*, vol. 7, *Two Essays on Analytical Psychology* (Princeton, N.J.: Princeton University Press, 1967).

night). And even though I was my paternal grandparents' only grandchild at the time and could get damn near anything out of them with a smile and a smooth "I love you," they weren't buying them either. So, after weeks and weeks of me trying to get some out of him, my dad finally deaded the conversation, shutting down the remotest of possibilities. But he did throw me a consolation prize. A lifeline to try and maintain the fragile struggle of "cool" that, in my mind, I was in danger of losing every day at school. My rubber and toxic-glue savior was the Magic Johnson Converse sneaker.

Magic's shoe was cool, sure. But back then nothing compared to Nike. Nike was young. It was swaggy. It was hip-hop. It was culture. And the Jordan brand ruled over all that was the Nike kingdom. So, while I was happy to walk the halls of Baty Elementary in Magic's shoes, they weren't the be-all and end-all.

One day, in the lunch line, Mikey and I heard a kid wearing Jordan 4s tell another kid that he was going to get the Jordan 5s because "they're so light, they make you float." Mikey didn't want my spoiled ass feeling down-and-out about my cool but nevertheless inferior sneakers; therefore he whispered in my ear, "I bet you yours float too." I looked back at him: "Prove it."

The only way to prove Mikey's hypothesis was to put it to a test. He suggested we throw my Magic Johnson Converse sneakers in the rain gutter behind the triplex base housing we lived in. No one at school ever busted on my shoes, but still, for me, I wanted to tell everyone that my shoes could float like Jordans too. And I always did like a good science experiment.

For the occasion, Mikey, dressed in his normal Cross Colours, had a lab coat draped over him and a pen and pad in his hands to take notes. When I took my Magic Johnson Converse sneakers off and flung them into the dirty, rushing river that was the rain gutter, Mikey pumped his fist in the air in excitement, like Michael Jordan hitting a game-winning jumper and busting Craig Ehlo's ankles. The shoes hit the water with a splash and before I knew it, they were moving! I tried running along the gutter but there was no rescue mission happening. They were gone.

That day I learned that Magic Johnson Converse sneakers could in fact float like Jordans. What little me didn't know was that most shoes with foam bottoms float. After a day or two of wearing my old shoes to school and around the house, my parents asked what happened to my Magic Johnson Converse sneakers. I told them about the experiment with the rain gutter and how it was Mikey's idea, but my dad wasn't buying "Mikey told me to do it." I spent the rest of the night in my room writing sentences. *I will not throw my shoes into the gutter.*

—

IN FOURTH GRADE, WHEN I WAS NINE, WE MOVED OFF BERGSTROM Air Force Base in South Austin into East Austin. East Austin used to be considered the hood. The local news would concentrate their broadcast journalism efforts on reporting about incidents that happened on the east side, even though there was as much if not more "crime" happening across other, "nicer" parts of the city. At the time, East Austin was where most of the Latin and Black populations in the city lived.

Today that same area is full of waterfront condos, a Soho House, and high-end vintage shops.

After ten or so years serving Uncle Sam, my dad was released from service when he busted his elbow. The Air Force told him he'd have to have a ton of surgeries to pull out all of the fragments that broke loose in his arm, and by the time he was forty he'd only have about 50 percent mobility in his elbow. So, he left the Air Force, took a job working at McDonnell Douglas (RIP), and moved us off-base to East Austin, near the river.

For the first time, we moved on from living in one-bedroom apartments and utilitarian base housing into a two-story duplex. We were like the Jeffersons, "moving on up to that duplex apartment on the East Siiiiiide." It was just at the end of my parents' means, though, so we did things to save money, like when it got cold we'd use the gas oven to heat the entire house, and because heat rises our rooms upstairs would be warm by the time we went to bed. (I know that flooding my place with the smell of natural gas is nauseating and headache-inducing and I'm sure not safe, but I still do this a couple times a year.)

That summer, before school started, while I was on my yearly pilgrimage to visit family in Sacramento, my aunt Shanice gave me an S-Curl, because my hair was nappy and matted due to my refusal to put product in it or brush it. I was fine with my hair the way it was. I liked rolling out of bed, ready to go. I kicked and screamed when she pushed me down in the wicker chair at my nana's table. After about forty-five minutes of her lathering my head in scalp-burning cream, washing it out, and layering my hair with gel, she finally let me look in the mirror. On sight, I stood taller. I felt like Billy Dee Williams—smooth and slick; I just knew that when I got back in school the girls would be all over me.

When I got back home to Austin that August, I wanted to keep my S-Curl up. Mikey assured me this was it; this would set us apart at school. My parents on the other hand didn't want me relaxing my hair and told me to cut it off "before your hair catch on fire," and to also stop putting blue Luster's S-Curl Activator Gel in my hair, because it was staining their couches. I ignored them; I was committed. To keep my S-Curl long and wavy, Shanice taught me to wear a durag every night. So, before bed, I'd sneak into the bathroom and squeeze an entire bottle of the blue gel into the palms of my hands, rub it in my hair and slick it back, and tie up the rag. I was about to be like Morris Day and the Time when I started school. "Is anybody hot? . . . No! . . . You know why? . . . Why? . . . 'Cuz I'm so COOL! Honey, baby can't you see . . ."

My hair was only the first layer of the new persona I was cultivating. Since I was starting at a new school, Mikey insisted I create a new airtight persona that everyone there would love. And since we noticed all the kids in my new neighborhood were Latin, we decided we should be Afro-Latin lovers. Duh!

The slick-backed, gel-heavy hair was only step one. The second step was to change my name. I'm named after my father, Wendell Romon Ellis Sr., and so I decided to go by my middle name, Romon. Name change: check. The last piece of my *muy grande* persona swap was locking in an accent. If I was going to be a Latin lover, I had to imitate the full and sensual sounds of the Romance languages, more specifically Spanish (again, I didn't say this plan was smart or politically correct).

Over 80 percent of the students at my new school spoke Spanish as their primary language. Therefore, the school administrators decided to place me, a non–Spanish speaker, in a class with the sixteen other kids who spoke English as their first language. While the rest of the school got to move around from classroom to classroom, us sixteen unrestrained and ill-disciplined non-Spanish-speaking kids had to sit in the same classroom for the entire day. It was like being locked in detention for eight hours. Trust me, I know why the caged bird sings. The one good thing about being on lockdown was that I only had to keep my Romon character up while I was in the cafeteria for lunch and on the playground for recess, since those were the only times we were around the rest of the kids. I just needed to keep it tight for forty-five minutes of an eight-and-a-half-hour day. Mikey had warned this wouldn't work—forty-five minutes of persona bait and switch—if I didn't go all in. One hundred percent. No days off. A lesson I still carry. So, I committed to Romon . . . and his accent.

Knowing that speaking Spanish was the most important part of the plan, Mikey and I watched Univision all day, every day. Whenever we were in the car, I'd ask my mom or dad to turn the radio station to a Latin station so I could try to sing along. We were trying to soak up as much of the language as possible, so that we could put Romon on full display at school. After two weeks of S-Curl activation and telenovela watching, I was ready to go. Romon was about to break hearts.

The night before the first day of school, I did my usual ritual of sneaking into the bathroom to gel my hair and tie it up. But over the previous week, I had also added in my newest nighttime ritual, crawling into bed and repeating the five or six Spanish words I'd learned while mixing in some "Spanish"-accented English, until I fell asleep. Mikey and I meticulously planned my outfit: black Nike Cortez, which I picked up in Sac over the summer (thanks to my aunt, who knew all things cool), paired with black, acid-washed Bugle Boy jeans and a San Francisco 49ers T-shirt—Niner Gang!

At the bus stop the next morning, Mikey quizzed me like we were prepping for a test.

"What do you say first?"

"*Hola,*" I replied. "Then I say *cake pasta?*"

Mikey violently shook his head. "Nooo, man. I know you're hungry but you gotta focus. *Que pasa.* You say, *Que pasa?*"

When the bus pulled up, Mikey and I climbed the stairs with our heads held high. Bravado on 100. Proud of my fit and my Billie Dee silky waves, I looked everyone in the eye. I slid into an empty row about midway through the rows of brown vinyl seats, while Mikey stayed on his feet surveying the crowd.

One of the kids across from me kept looking at me out of the corner of his eye. It was the thing kids do when they're shy and want to talk to you, but don't want to be the first to speak. I looked over my shoulder at Mikey and he shook his head no, but the bus hit a bump so I thought he was nodding up and down as if to say, *Put that Spanish to work!*

Hair slicked back and chest puffed out, I turned to the kid and let it go: "*Que pasta?*"

It took seconds for them to decimate me.

"What's your name?" someone asked.

EASY! I knew to roll the hell out of my *r*'s.

"Romon," I said, with perfect pronunciation, puckered lips and all. There was a beat of quiet. I exhaled; I thought my pronunciation and accent had thrown them off.

"What kind of accent is that?"

I used my best accent: *"Ezpenhole."* A few kids giggled.

"Where are you from?"

"Yo donna South Carolina," I said. Two kids in front of me laughed so hard I'm sure their stomachs ached for the rest of the day.

"You don't speak Spanish, *idiota."*

I turned to Mikey, who was now violently shaking his head: *Nooooooo.* He sank behind the seat, and I followed suit; praying that the kids would find something else to move on to. Twenty—quietly praying—minutes later we pulled up in front of the school. I waited for everyone else to get off, hoping that I'd go unseen if I got off last. After the last kids got up, Mikey looked at me and said, "I think we should kill Romon." When I stepped off that bus I was Jay again. But for the next four months, every time I got on the bus in the morning, all the kids asked, "Where's Romon?"

MIKEY MAY HAVE HAD INTERESTING METHODS OF HELPING ME FIT in and feel less alone—some that may have been the basis for my love of performing today—but his antics helped color my world, gave me refuge from the monotony of moving and the torment of growing up. We rarely had a dull moment. And we may have almost made my hand fall off from all the sentences I had to write, but it was worth it.

THE WEEK I JOINED A GANG

"I knew I had the bubble guts for a reason."

B Y THE TIME I WAS IN MIDDLE SCHOOL, MOST EVERYTHING I knew about gangs came from three previous gang-related experiences, none of which were particularly alluring, and yet at the ripe age of fourteen, I decided to join a gang.

If anyone asks what the appeal of a gang is, the answer, when you're a middle school kid in a new city in a new school looking for your new friend group, is easy: What's not appealing? You get a built-in group of friends, you always get chosen for a team during pickup games, someone always has your back when things go down, you spend less time picking out clothes because you wear one color, and lastly, you get to start your own enterprise.

It took one week, seven days, for me to understand what's *not* appealing.

—

My first experience with gangs wasn't "in the streets" as mainstream media at the time would make you believe. It was at my favorite place to go, the idyllic safe haven known as the Century Domes Theater in Sacramento, California. Three futuristic space-age domes made up the Jetsons-style beacon, built to hold the marvels of filmmaking.

Mikey and I spent the summer of 1991 in Sacramento ping-ponging back and forth between my grandparents' houses. Booker and Barbara (my paternal grandparents) lived just a few blocks away from Joetta (my maternal grandma)— who rebranded herself "Nana" because she thought she was too young to let me call her Grandma in front of people. All of them had settled in Sacramento because of McClellan Air Force Base, which was just outside of Sac. My paternal grandfather, Booker; my maternal grandfather, James; and my step-grandfather, Gene, were all Air Force enlistees who'd found themselves stationed at McClellan at one time or another. Nana moved into her house around the corner from my dad's parents just after my mom started high school, where my parents met, fell in love, and at eighteen and nineteen conceived yours truly.

Each of my parents is one of three children, with their youngest siblings, my mom's sister and my dad's brother, being a lot younger than my mom and dad. My mom's sister, Shanice, is about nine years older than me, so in many ways she was like the cool big sister I never had. She ran with a group of friends who stayed dressed in graffitied denim, she always knew the latest music and dances, and she was on the cheerleading team. She was "cool like that," rah-rah and dignified all at the same time. Whenever I stayed with her and Nana, I would beg to tag along with my aunt in whatever she was doing that day. Whether it was bowling, walking around the Old Sac Waterfront, or going to play miniature golf, I stayed by her side like Mikey did mine. Therefore, during the literal and metaphorical hot summer of '91, when Shanice made plans to see *Boyz N the Hood* with her boyfriend, it was no different.

"I gotta figure what I'ma tell Momma," I overheard Shanice whispering on the phone. Mikey and I popped our heads around the kitchen corner, finding Shanice bouncing around on her feet, twirling the long yellow phone cord around her finger. Whoever she was talking to, she was sprung. She was standing in the doorway between the kitchen and the garage, with her back to the kitchen so her voice wouldn't travel into the house where my nana, with superhuman hearing, was. Shanice looked over her shoulder in my direction as if she could feel me spying on her, and eyed me. Mikey and I popped back behind the wall to hide.

"I'll see you later . . . You stupid. I'll be there. Okay. Bye." Shanice connected the yellow phone back to the yellow base hanging on the wall. Her feet moved across the kitchen floor so fast I thought she was on Marty McFly's hoverboard. I didn't have time to react—seriously, I think she floated.

"Why you in my business?" she said, while reaching her hand around the wall and grabbing me.

"I'm not!" I blurted out. "Let me go." I tried to pull away, but my prepubescent noodle arms were no match for her superhuman cheerleading strength. "Let me go . . . Nana! Nana!" She quickly let go. Shanice feared nothing . . . except Nana.

"Be quiet. Shhhh. I let you go." She towered over me as I glared up at her. Mikey leaned into my ear and whispered,

"Tell her you know what she was whispering about and you wanna go." My eyes quickly moved to the left to steal a glance at Mikey.

"I know what you were whispering 'bout to your friend and I wanna go too," I said, while defiantly locking eyes with Shanice. Fire surged out of her nose like a flamethrower.

"What? I'm not taking you nowhere. Get out my face and go sit down somewhere, boy."

"I'll tell Nana—"

Shanice grabbed me before I could finish. Mikey backed against the wall and murmured, "Uh-oh."

"You not going to say nothing to Nana and I'm not taking you—"

"Where you not taking him?" Nana asked. Shanice dropped my arm and Mikey leaned off the wall. Shanice and I both turned toward Nana with blank looks on both our faces. Like Shanice, Nana also floated.

"Hello!" Nana said, sucking her teeth, "My God. Y'all acting like y'all deaf. Did you hear me? Where do you want her to take you?"

Shanice and I, for completely different reasons, gulped in full synchronicity. I looked at Shanice, who I could tell was trying to think of a lie but couldn't. Her nostrils flared, while her eyes pleaded for me to not rat her out and mess up her plans. I quickly looked at Mikey, who was acting out something . . . *to go to the* . . . Mikey squeezed his hands together like he was yanking a joystick. He threw his arms over his right shoulder down toward the ground like he was swinging at something. He was working hard. He balled up his right fist and made a tossing motion with his arm. Video games. Whac-A-Mole. Skee-Ball.

". . . To the arcade to play games," I said, hesitantly. Nana and Shanice both turned toward me. Nana's eyebrows squished together like they were fighting for space.

"Why can't you take him to the arcade? Hmm? You don't have nothing else to do."

Shanice paused for a beat. "I was going to—"

Nana cut Shanice off: "Get my pocketbook so I can give you some money."

Shanice, surprised, darted out of the room—Nana never handed out money, and Shanice wasn't about to question it.

Nana looked at me. "She'll take you, baby, and if she got anybody with her, you tell me what happens when you get back home. Okay?"

This was a setup. Nana wanted me to snitch on Shanice. Mikey looked at me with one of those smiles you make when you're nervous and don't know what to say, so you just grin and nod your head up and down really fast. So I looked at Nana and did the same.

LATER THAT EVENING, SHANICE AND I PILED INTO NANA'S GOLD Nissan and started the drive across town, but we didn't get very far before our first stop.

"I've gotta pick up a friend," Shanice said while turning off Walerga Road and making a right into a residential neighborhood. We drove a few blocks with her looking out the window, reading the house numbers under her breath until she slammed on the brakes in front of a peach-colored stucco triplex. She honked twice and told me to "get in the back." I unbuckled and started to crawl my way between the seats to the back, until I felt her pull at my legs, "Uh-uh! Go around."

A few seconds later the door of one of the triplex units opened and out came Shanice's friend dressed in faded jeans, Chuck Taylors, and a letterman jacket.

"Don't tell Nana we picked Devin up, okay?" Before I could respond, Devin was already opening the door, falling into *my* front seat, and kissing Shanice. Mikey gagged and fake-spit.

"What up, lil man?" Devin said as he looked over his shoulder and nodded his head. I didn't speak; instead I just sat salty, watching him get comfortable in my seat.

"Say hi," Shanice demanded. I stared at her. "Whatever. Don't pay no attention to him," she told Devin. "My momma made me bring him." Shanice dropped the car in drive and Devin turned up the radio.

I STILL DIDN'T KNOW WHERE WE WERE ACTUALLY GOING, BUT about fifteen minutes of West Coast rap mixed with Naughty by Nature and Salt-N-Pepa (two of the few East Coast groups allowed on West Coast radio at the time) later, we arrived at our destination. The Century Domes Theater was *the* spot to see any new movie in Sac. There were three theaters, each with a sparkling white dome roof. The parking lot was full of activity. Police officers stood watch in cars, on foot, and on horseback. Before we got out of the car, Devin looked toward Shanice.

"You not wearing any colors, right?" She shook her head no. *That's a full lie,* I thought. Shanice was dressed in head-to-toe graffitied denim. There were tons of colors spray-painted on her pants and jacket. "What about lil man?" They both looked back at me, eyes wide.

"Of course I'm wearing colors. Duh. What else would I be wearing?"

"Are you wearing red or blue?" she asked. Mikey and I both did a quick once-over and answered in unison, "No."

"Let's go then," she said, opening the door. "And don't talk to nobody you don't know."

Mikey rolled his eyes as we all hopped out of the car. "She can't tell us who to talk to. Who she think she is, Nana?" he said.

In the parking lot, groups of men, both young and grown, stood near Impalas, Coupe de Villes, Cadillac Fleetwoods, and Chevy Novas. It was like a car show. Some of the guys were smoking and drinking. Some just chilling. And others posturing. One part parking-lot pimping. One part marking their territory. Bass from the sound systems rattled across the asphalt, making the five hairs on my arm stand up. Each car we passed bumped a different West Coast classic: "Quik Is the Name," "Death Certificate," "Niggaz 4 Life."

The summer's humidity, mixed with the sodium vapor orange parking-lot lights, made everyone glow. All the homeys in that lot looked like royalty, laid with gold chains, cars, and status. To a young boy who loved cars and rap, it felt cool. It felt inviting. There was an allure to it that made it feel like a place you belonged, or at least a place you wanted to belong.

"Come on," Mikey said, trailing behind Shanice and Devin, who walked with purpose, never breaking stride, toward the ticket office. Mikey wanted to kick it with the homeys, but even if he didn't like Shanice's attitude, he appreciated her focus. Also, he wasn't trying to catch her fade.

When we arrived at the ticket office, Devin quickly handed over the money as he asked for three tickets to *Boyz N the Hood*. The braces-faced, teenage salesclerk—just trying to get through his summer job—tepidly handed over the tickets. Mikey clocked the clerk acting funny.

"I've seen that look before . . . Something ain't right," Mikey said. It didn't connect until much later, but Mikey was right. The clerk's darting eyes and shaking hands should have been an omen as to what the night had in store.

The entryway of the theater was packed—people were hanging out, buying snacks, posted-up cops skulked in every corner, hands at their weapons. Shanice squeezed my hand so tight I swear I could feel my bones folding on themselves. Mikey reminded me, "We passed a paramedic in the parking lot if she broke it. You'll be good!"

Shanice held on to me as we made our way through the crowd and into our assigned theater. The screen was massive and slightly curved; it wrapped around the far walls of the theater. Fractals of light from high above filtered through the air from the three different cameras pointing at the screen. Nearly every red faux velvet seat was filled.

"Excuse me . . . My bad," Shanice and Devin were saying as we shuffled around and stepped over people. They were on their best behavior, and Mikey and I did everything we could to trail behind them. By accident, I kicked over someone's popcorn that was sitting on the floor. "Aye, lil nigg—" Shanice jumped in: "Sorry about that. Here's some money for another one." She handed the guy a few dollars and yanked me along.

The crowd in the theater was very visibly split into a few different groups. There were people who wore red or blue; people affiliated with those who wore red or blue but didn't wear those colors themselves; and then there were people like us, who wore neutral colors or ridiculous shades of green, yellow, orange, probably to not be confused with red or blue. The groups didn't intermingle. Folks sat with their people regardless of the seat number printed on their ticket stub.

There was something in the air that I couldn't identify, but I felt its deafening presence. It was suffocating, like the humidity of an El Niño–hot Sacramento summer day, and it threatened to spill over, like anything could happen at any time. It felt like a lack of control; a lack of safety. I didn't know it then but do now—it was a fierce tension.

Shanice looked over to me. "You don't need to go to the bathroom, right? 'Cause once the movie starts, we not moving."

I shook my head no, but Mikey leaned in and said, "I think I might have to go. I got the bubble guts." Bubble guts was a sign of nervousness for Mikey. Usually, whenever he had them, he was in a high-stress situation that he had no control over. It was his body's way of saying: *Something ain't right, bruh!*

Before I could tell Shanice, Mikey started coughing from the weed smoke that floated through the air like a butterfly gently weaving itself around the theater. Mikey tried to identify what was burning by taking a few big inhales.

"It smells like burning grass. No idea why someone would smoke that. Especially indoors where there's hardly any ventilation," he said. After a few more inhales and a few more coughs, an easy smile stretched across his face. He leaned back, and relaxed into his seat.

The house lights flickered, signaling the film's imminent start, and the crowd began to quiet down. Some of them.

When the theater reached pitch-black someone yelled, "Y'all betta shut the fuck up 'fore I come up there and shut you up!"

"You ain't gon' do shit," echoed up from the front of the theater. Flashlights blinked on and two officers pointed them into the sea of Black and brown faces.

"If we need to remove anyone from the theater, we will gladly do so," one officer said while scanning the crowd. They turned their flashlights off just as the opening credit sequence began.

"Sit yo' ol' square rent-a-cop ass down somewhere!" someone in the back yelled, and in a brief moment of unity everyone in the theater burst out laughing—except the officers, they were in their feelings.

As the voiceover started to play over the opening cards of the movie, everyone quieted down again. The intensity of the scene captivated the entire theater. *"Fuck that . . . Where my strap? . . . I'm finna let 'em have it"* POP POP POP. A few people in the crowd jumped at the gunfire ringing from the screen. It sounded a little too real. After a beat, there appeared onscreen the chyron and a red stop sign: "One out of every twenty-one Black American males will be murdered in their lifetime."

The theater was silent. The camera began a stunningly slow push into the red stop sign and I was taken. The homeys seemed more concerned about their seats, the girls with them, and peacocking for the other cliques than they were about reading John Singleton's message. But I felt like I was seeing myself onscreen walking to school every morning . . . that is, until Tre took his friends to see the murder scene. Gunshots rang out over the Ronald Reagan FOUR MORE YEARS poster, which incited boos and "Reagan ain't shit!" "Get his ass off the screen!" People snickered and laughed, but it felt far away; I had already sunk into that world.

I watched as the camera panned over walls of the on-screen classroom covered with elementary drawings that depicted kids' home situations. Kids were asleep on their desks, and an out-of-touch teacher who looked nothing like the students taught them a history scrubbed clean of the contributions of their very culture. I could smell the Blue Magic in the boys' short hair, and the Mane 'n Tail in the girls' perfectly braided hair. I could hear the boys whispering back and forth, bemoaning their boredom. I saw myself in that classroom, which was eerily similar to my own.

Onscreen, we watched a series of cascading events: Ricky getting bumped by Ferris, a Blood; Ferris firing a machine gun into the air; and Ricky getting shot by one of Ferris's guys. The tension in the theater became palpable again. People shifted in their seats and started yelling at the screen, and then yelling at each other. Popcorn and drinks flew through the air. Threats and insults hurled across the dark space. Officers shined their flashlights. Within seconds, people were jumping over seats and swinging at each other.

"See me then," a Blood yelled. Across the theater a Crip in a Dodgers hat responded by throwing a soda at him, but it hit another guy wearing a herringbone chain. Herringbone ran down the far aisle with the same speed the soda had traveled through the air and hit his chest.

"He's got a gun!" someone on our right screamed. If chaos hadn't already erupted, it sure as hell did after that. People started screaming. Officers squawked into their walkies for backup. Non-affiliated people stampeded toward the doors. Shanice grabbed my hand and pulled me as she fought to get out of our row. For a second I lost Mikey in the melee.

"Stay with me! Don't stop running!" Shanice yelled at the top of her lungs. The lights in the theater, having been off and needing to warm up, were slowly fading up.

"Drop your weapon!" one officer yelled with his revolver out, pointing into the crowd. The Crip did not drop his weapon; instead he raised his gun in the air and shot. *POP POP POP!* Bullets hummed through the space with deep bass like a deacon mid–church service on a Sunday afternoon. White dust from the ceiling fell like fake snow at a cheap North Pole setup in Florin Mall. The crowd exploded, shrieks piercing through the air. Mikey pushed his way through the crowd screaming, "I don't wanna go out like this!" Shanice bulldozed a few people and pushed us into the lobby.

The fight had oozed its way there as well. There were gang homeys from the parking lot coming into the theater. Now sandwiched between the fight erupting out of the theater and the people fighting to get into the lobby, Shanice and Devin had to find a new way to get us out. To the left was the concession stand, and to the right were the restrooms and stairs to the projection room. We had one choice. Shanice bent over and yelled, "Stay low and don't let go of my hand!" When a stand-up movie poster for *Rocketman* went flying through the air, Mikey got the message and bent over as well.

Devin pulled up the rear as Shanice pushed us through, around, and in between other people trying to get out. We were inches away from two pairs of sneakers crashing down and stomping a guy who lay on the ground in a ball trying to minimize the trauma as he took stomps to his midsection and head. Shanice had a hand on the door to outside, and could barely squeeze it open because of the fighting on the other side. She held it ajar, just enough so I could crawl through her legs and get out. Once Mikey and I were through, Shanice and Devin popped out. The cops on foot and on horse tried to contain the outside edges of the fights taking place right in front of the theater doors. *POP POP POP POP!* Shots went off and everyone dove to the heat-radiating cement for cover. Shanice pulled me to the ground. When the shooting stopped, we ran toward the parking lot. A cop on horseback was to our right and we watched him hit a man in a wheelchair, who wore all red, with his baton. The Blood in the wheelchair flipped over, and he was struggling to pull himself up with only his arms.

To our left a K-9 unit of German shepherds were goaded into attacking everyone in front of them. A man who was being attacked by one of the dogs pulled a gun from his waist. He twisted left and right as the dog clamped its jaw down on his leg and twisted him around. After a few beats of scrambling, the man got a shot off and hit the dog. In an instant, officers drew their weapons and shot the man. His gun fell to the ground as he grabbed his shoulder, screaming in pain. The officers flipped him on his stomach and cuffed him, while blood spilled out of him.

Shanice dragged me across the parking lot with Mikey running full sprint behind. In all the pandemonium and chaos, it took us a beat to find the car, but when we did, the factory gold paint on my nana's Nissan never shined so bright.

Devin shoved me in the back seat while Shanice dove into the driver's seat. As soon as Devin got in, Shanice punched the gas and peeled out of the parking lot. *POP POP POP POP*

POP! We heard more gunfire, and Shanice drove faster. Mikey and I smooshed our faces against the back window as we drove away from what had turned into a small riot.

Mikey huffed and puffed his way through a few strained breaths and then whispered to himself, "I knew I had the bubble guts for a reason."

—

STOCKTON, CALIFORNIA, IN THE '90S WAS A SANCTUARY FOR GANG activity. For most of the decade it was ranked both the number-one most violent city in California and one of the ten most violent cities in the United States.

Every day, especially in the summer—heat makes real G's cranky—there were not just stories on the news but also stories from my aunts, uncles, or cousins who witnessed something going down firsthand.

My great-aunt Bettina—loud, boisterous, fun, loving, but she could also put the fear of God in you when she raised her hand—wouldn't even wear her wedding band when she left the house. Not because she was creeping on my great-uncle Howard but because while at a gas station, one of her friends got two of her fingers cut off because two dudes—not even in masks—ran up on her at the pump wanting her to run the jewels. My aunt's friend had swollen hands, so the rings didn't slide off easily. They cut a finger off each hand to get a couple hundred dollars' worth of gold.

Being a young boy back then was a mindf$*k! On one hand, you admired the gangs, you looked up to some of the members, and you wanted to be in a group that protected its own. On the other hand, you hated how neighborhoods were being torn apart, you were terrified you were going to be in the wrong place at the wrong time, and you never knew who to trust. Even though I was mad impressionable and wasn't always sure which way was up, I always felt grounded when I was in Stockton because of my cousin Marcus.

Marcus was as charismatic as President Obama. He had a smile that could light up a room—partially because of his gold tooth. He had a cool, raspy voice and was always telling jokes. He was fun to be around and made every barbecue better—that is, until he made them worse.

One summer, while in Sacramento with Nana, we piled in the car and made the very hot drive—no AC and windows rolled up because of cow pasture methane—down the I-5 to Stockton. We frequently took these weekend trips, which for me consisted of being tortured by my cousins; having to take a bath with my cousins to conserve my aunt's water bill; sleeping in one room with my cousins; being called all of my cousins' names before my aunt finally remembered mine ("AishaPatriciaSameera—boyyouknowI'mtalkingtoyou—Wendell Jr."); a Saturday barbecue, because "you gotta get on up, yeah you can't sit down" (Jodeci); church on Sunday mornings—my uncle Kevin gives the longest sanctified filled-with-the-Holy-Ghost sermons on the planet; and finally, after eating the barbecue's leftovers, getting back in Nana's gold Nissan Sentra to endure the long drive back to Sac.

The highlight was always the Saturday barbecue. We'd go to the park with Styrofoam coolers filled with marinated meats wrapped in foil, skewers of vegetables, greens, potato salad, corn on the cob, baked beans, sodas—this side of the family called 'em "pop" because they're originally from

Ohio—and wine coolers for the grown folk. My uncle, always one for betting, brought dominoes and cards because, as he would say, "I'm taking somebody money today!" Someone brought speakers and us kids ran to the playground. The park was a vibe.

When the food was ready we all crowded around a table and held hands while my uncle Kevin blessed the meal—the first of his never-ending prayers for the weekend. My legs tingled as they started to go numb, like when you sit with your legs crossed for too long, and as the seconds became minutes, Mikey leaned over: "Is Jesus coming back today? 'Cause if not, the flies gon' get on the chicken before this prayer is over." As I looked up to the sky, a ray of sunshine filtered its way through the trees above and warmed my face. "In Jesus' name, Amen!" God granted me a miracle. The end of the longest praying over food in Oak Grove Park history.

After stuffing our faces with everything on the table, Mikey and I liked to watch my uncle Howard's spades game. My uncle loved to trash-talk and get under people's skin while he was taking their money. He had to let people know how he was "busting they be-hinds." The real problem is, by that point in the day all the adults had had a few too many St. Ides, so nobody wanted to hear what he had to say while he was digging in their pockets.

Marcus, in New Testament style, showed up to the park later than everyone else, blasting "Black Superman" through the two 15-inch subwoofers in his trunk. He was beating up the block while smoke billowed from his half-rolled-down window. "Now everybody sing, 'BLACK SUPERMAN'!" He hopped out of the car in baggy oversized jeans, a white shirt that was a few sizes too big for him, and black Locs shades.

Usually everybody loved Marcus. He was the life of every party, but this time, when he approached the family, the mood shifted. Mikey tilted his head, clocking it first: "Something is a lil off." No one said "What's up?," handed him a beer, or told him to jump in on the electric slide. Instead everyone turned their backs, continued their conversations, and made as little eye contact as possible. A few even kissed the back of their teeth. Still, Marcus made his rounds, speaking to most everyone. He made his way to the basketball court, where he threw up a few shots, then swayed up to the spades table and posted up.

"What's up, Marcus?" I said as he walked by. Marcus looked in my direction.

"You must want something?"

"I was just saying what's up," I replied.

"I heard you," he said with a smirk, knowing I wanted to sneak a sip of his beer.

The first few hands at the spades table went quickly. On each round, the team playing against Marcus's got the exact number of books they bid. Marcus was frustrated.

"You biddin' too many," he told his teammate, another cousin.

"Get out my hand, bruh. I know what I'm doing!"

"Make us lose again and see what happen then."

Meanwhile my uncle Howard, the Oak Grove Park resident shit-talker, was feeling himself and couldn't help but jump in.

"Y'all gon' lose 'cause y'all some little boys trying to play a grown man's game." Never in the history of ever has any grown man been okay with someone calling him "little" or a "boy." You're damn near better off talking about his mom than calling him "little" or a "boy." The cousin on Marcus's team started laughing. "He talking to yo' ass 'cause I ain't no little—" *BOOM!* Before he could finish his sentence his face violently met the metal picnic table. Blood trickled down his nose while his eyes tried to focus.

"Say I'm a little boy again," Marcus evenly said, still seated next to him as if he hadn't just slammed someone's head into a table. He lowered his head slightly, pushing his eyebrows together in a challenging stance. "Say that shit."

Everyone in the park froze. Marcus had a look in his eyes I'd never seen before. His big hands slapped the cards off the table and he finished the last of his backwashed Mad Dog as he stood up. "Come over here and get some," he said, challenging whoever looked in his direction. Uncle Howard popped up from the table. Mikey was pulling at my shoulder, but I was transfixed.

"All that ain't necessary. The hell is wrong with you?" my uncle yelled. Aunt Bettina stormed over. Standing in Marcus's face.

"You gon' hit me? Huh?" she asked.

"Man, get out my face with that."

My uncle seethed. "I don't know what has gotten into you and what them fools you running with got you thinking but this right here"—pointing at the picnic table—"this ain't it. Ain't no Bloods or Crips or what'n'ever else you into out there, here in this family."

Marcus's bloodshot eyes rolled from side to side, calculating. A long tense beat passed before he said, "I'm out." He casually walked to his car like nothing had happened, stopping to dig in the cooler for another Mad Dog before hopping in his ride and turning up his system. Eazy-E's voice echoed through the park, "He was once a thug from around the way," as Marcus punched the gas and sped away.

TWO SUMMERS LATER—WE'D SKIPPED THE PREVIOUS SUMMER BE- cause we had just moved to Oklahoma—Mikey and I went back to Cali. We pulled up to my aunt and uncle's house to find my uncle finishing a ramp over the steps to the front door.

"He here yet?" Nana asked as we made our way from the car to the house.

"Nah. Not yet, 'posed to be here any minute," my uncle responded without looking up. Rubber-handled hammer pounding in the last gray nail on his ramp. Nana looked at me.

"Boy, what's wrong with you? You can't speak? Say hi to your uncle."

If I could have spoken freely, I probably would have said: *Yes, I can speak, but you were just talking and if I talked over you, you would have slapped me across the back of my head. So I waited. And now you're telling me I should have spoken. Do you realize how confusing this is?*

Instead I said, "Hi, Unc'," as Mikey and I moved into the house. Inside, all my cousins sat in front of the TV watching reruns of *Press Your Luck*. They yelled at the TV, hardly notic- ing I was there. I could tell Just For Me had just been applied to their hair, because the room smelled like it mixed with "beans, greens, potatoes, tomatoes, lamb, ram—you name it!" It was a Shirley Caesar kind of day. This wasn't normal. I'd never gone down to Stockton on a non-Sunday and walked into a full buffet at my great-aunt and -uncle's house. We only got a bountiful spread like this if it was after church, a pre-planned cookout, or a special occasion.

The distinct notes of barbecue sauce, smoke seasoning, fatback, and Lawry's seasoned salt wafting through the air made my stomach RUMBLE. Mikey grabbed my shoulder. His eyelids flapped closed while he inhaled the scents of my uncle's bomb-ass "famous" barbecue sauce. I know there are many forms of torture and I'm not trivializing nor downplaying any of them, but for a young boy, aka a trash compactor, smelling food you can't eat—because you know if you do, one of the aunties will hit you so hard you'll get "knocked back into the civil rights movement"—is very high on the torture list.

As tempted as I was, I wasn't trying to revisit the past that day. Plus the unsettling feeling I had, not knowing what was going on and why everyone was so quiet, competed for my stomach's attention. I felt uneasy and started to realize my cousins were shifting uncomfortably and whispering—they were nervous.

Instead of trying to sneak food, Mikey and I tried to stealthily find out why everyone was acting like we were waiting for Dr. King to come out of his grave and over for dinner. We plopped down on the floor next to the cousins. I looked over at the cousins, not sure which one to probe for information first because they all lived by the same code: "Snitches get stitches and end up in ditches." But I knew one of them couldn't help herself—Sameera was too honest. Normally a great virtue but for me an easy mark. She would rather tell you not to tell anyone than lie to you, so I crawled my way through the girls and scooted next to her.

"Hey."

She turned to look at me. "Ugh. You stink. What's that smell?"

I was a musty boy, what can I say. "That's not me . . . that's . . . that's . . ." I whispered really low: "I think Aisha forgot to take a shower."

She rolled her eyes at me. "Whatchu want? I'm trying to watch the— No whammy!" She got distracted for a second.

Mikey and I quickly looked around to make sure no one was listening, then I leaned in to whisper in her ear, "Why's everyone acting all weird, and why is Unc' building a ramp?"

"You don't know?" she said, eyes wide. The vertebrae in my neck creaked as I twisted my head from left to right; Mikey twisted his right to left. She stood up and said, "Come on." Mikey and I quickly followed her to the entryway of the house. She stretched her neck around to make sure no one was nearby.

"You don't know what's happening today?"

Eating food, I hoped as my stomach made another grumbling noise. "I mean I figured it was probably somebody's birthday or something but everybody is acting all weird and quiet."

She shook her head no.

"Well then what is it?"

She looked at me for a beat, deciding if she wanted to tell me or not. I could see the inner turmoil dancing in her eyes. She was conflicted. And like most kids—and imaginary friends— with a secret, she couldn't hold it.

"Well, right after the last time you were here, I think, Marcus got in trouble with that gang he was in. Like selling drugs and robbing people. Momma said he even had a gun. Anyway, Grandma [my great-aunt] wouldn't let him come to the house no more because she said she didn't want that foolish s-h-i-t in her house. So, nobody heard from him for a few months. Then one day the cops busted into Grandma's house saying they were looking for him, but she didn't know where he was. A few days later, Grandpa [my great-uncle] got a call that the police had got Marcus but he was in the hospital."

"Hospital? They beat him up?" I asked.

"No. Well probably, yeah, but he also jumped out a car—"

"He jumped out the WHAT?!" She only heard one of us, but Mikey and I both blurted it out.

She yanked my arm—"Shhhh!"—and quickly whipped around again to verify were still alone. "He was in a car with the FBI man on the highway. Marcus didn't trust him and thought something was off when he tried to buy drugs off him. He pulled his gun and the FBI man told him he was arrested. So, Marcus jumped out the car while it was going like seventy miles per hour on the highway."

MY. JAW. WAS. ON. THE. FLOOR! I had so many questions. "Is he alive? Is he in jail? What happened after? Did he get away?"

"He was in the hospital for a long time but he lived. My momma went to go see him a few times. They thought he was going to get better and then go to prison but he's in a wheelchair and Grandma said he don't really speak right."

"Speak right?" Mikey and I looked at each other as she nodded her head, yes.

"He's coming home today and they're supposed to drop him off. That's why my grandpa had to build the ramp."

Just then Uncle burst through the door, "He's here, y'all!" Everyone in the house made their way out into the front yard. Still thrown by Sameera's discombobulating news, I stood inside the doorway and watched as the Department of Corrections bus opened its side door and slowly lowered my cousin in his wheelchair, down to the curb. Sameera looked back at me and said, "You can't tell nobody I told you."

She ran outside, leaving Mikey and me behind. We stood quiet for a beat. "Should we be sad or is that bad?" Mikey asked under his breath.

"I dunno? I mean . . . maybe not. He's still alive and maybe he stopped doing bad things. Also, he drove a really cool car," I said.

"Yeah, but don't look like he's driving anymore," Mikey said, eyes looking out to Marcus.

I was sad. I was heartbroken and confused. It was devastating that Marcus had lost his mobility and would forever need someone to help him with everyday tasks, but I was also crushed that my cousin as I knew him, as we all knew him, was gone. No more jokes. No more card games. No more sneaking me sips of beer when the aunties weren't looking. No more barbecues. Whatever happened while he ran with his gang took him away from us. Marcus, who had been a beacon of light in our family, had lost his flame.

—

MY THIRD AND FINAL GANG-RELATED EXPERIENCE—BEFORE I DEcided to join one myself—took place when I was about seven years old in Youngstown, Ohio, aka the City of You, aka YO. It's a city I always grew up referring to the same way all of my family who lived there did; as one of the devil's armpits. It is also one of the few places my mom's family has called home for five or six generations. Today it's on a journey to becoming a beautiful, revitalized Midwestern town with a strong, close-knit community—so says the city website—but when Mikey and I spent time there, it was very different.

Youngstown was originally a mill town. Deep in the Rust Belt, from the onset Youngstown manufactured steel, and as the industry began to take a downturn, so did the city. The loss of industry led to the decline of jobs, services, and resources and the rise of robbery, murders, and gang activity. In peak position, the Morgan Quitno Press ranked Youngstown as the ninth most dangerous city in the United States. At various points, Youngstown was given the nicknames "Murdertown, USA," "Crimetown, USA," and "Bomb City, USA." Newspapers used "Youngstown tune-up" as a slang term for any car-bomb assassinations. And although you could get the business pretty much anywhere in the city, the area hardest hit was where my great-grandmother, Big Ma, lived.

BIG MA HAD A FULL-ASS LIFE. ORIGINALLY FROM ALABAMA, SHE married at sixteen and had six kids. She kept a garden with greens, okra, beans, lettuce, and more that she cooked from every week. For a while she was a real-estate maven—buying and selling houses in her neighborhood to Black families. Big Ma had so many grandkids and great-grandkids that you'd be honored if she remembered your name—even if it was her twenty-second guess. She was always up at 6:00 A.M., cooked eggs and bacon every morning, smoked cigarettes, and "Shhhit"—with the longest *h* you ever heard—was her favorite word. She never missed a Bible study, and every Sunday she went to church like her life depended on it.

Her big laugh would fill up the entire house. She also had this amazing mystical power where if she dreamed of fish, it meant someone in our family was pregnant; it never failed.

One summer, my cousin Destiny, Mikey, and I went with Nana to Big Ma's house in Ohio thinking we were going to spend most of the month melting and sticking to her vinyl-covered floral couch.

Instead, this particular Youngstown summer getaway surprised us all.

One night, long after we had passed out from a day where Big Ma woke us up at six in the morning to clean, tend her garden, and get whooped in the basement for talking back, we were woken up by sobs and screams from downstairs. My cousin, Mikey, and I all wiped our eyes and stumbled out of bed. The three of us edged to the top of the narrow stairway and listened to the grown folk downstairs.

One of our older cousins and his homeboy had parked in front of the house after a night out. His homeboy was dropping him off, and as they dapped each other up, saying their goodbyes, sitting in his car, another car came down the street in the opposite direction and slowed to a crawl. The windows rolled down on the passenger side of the car as it pulled up parallel to the driver's side of my cousin's car.

Apparently a passenger in the other car yelled, "Aye!" before emptying a full clip in my cousin and his homeboy's direction. As neighbors heard the gunshots and turned on their porch lights in order to see outside, the car sped off into the night. It wasn't a Youngstown tune-up, but it was pretty close.

My cousin passed before any emergency responders made it to his side. His homeboy, covered in his blood, screamed and fled. Although nine rounds were shot into the car, he didn't get hit with a single bullet. To this day, he's never told his side of the story and never helped the detectives with their investigation.

Big Ma held it together, like she always did. As the matriarch of our family, she dug into her role as comforter, caregiver, and organizer. Never getting a chance to let her own pain and grief show. "You two," she told two of my aunts, "get over to Shante's house and make sure she's not alone. Tell her Pat and I will take care of planning the funeral tomorrow morning. Daren, grab my pocketbook from upstairs and go to the store to get them some groceries. Bruh, hand me my phone book so I can call round to the police station and see what I can find out. Alright, y'all go on."

The cops never arrested the men responsible for the murder. But the detectives covering the case had a theory that my cousin's homeboy was actually the target for the hit and that's why he never talked.

—

YOU MAY BE THINKING AT THIS POINT, *AFTER HAVING EXPERIENCED all that, why would anyone try to be in a gang?* I stand by the points I made earlier, the most important of which is that a gang provided me with a built-in community during a time I felt exhausted from looking for new friends after yet another move. I was thirteen and Mikey was less and less present. I was on my own, and this was a solution.

DAY ONE

I SPENT THE END OF MIDDLE SCHOOL THROUGH HIGH SCHOOL IN the Green Country city that gave us national treasures Alfre Woodard; Garth Brooks's "The Thunder Rolls"; Etan Thomas, who until Ja Morant rocked the best dreadlocks in NBA history; John Starks, who dunked on you know who; James "Quick" Tillis, the first man to go twelve rounds with Mike Tyson; all-time Top Five *SNL* cast member Bill Hader; Hanson ("MMMbop" gets stuck in my head once a month); and finally, the Gap Band, whose name stood for Greenwood, Archer, and Pine, the same three streets that Black Wall Street occupied until the 1921 Greenwood massacre, and my morning bus route to George Washington Carver Middle School in none other than Tulsa, Oklahoma.

My family moved to the south side of town and I went to a magnet school forty-five minutes away on the north side. Every morning I'd wake up as late as possible, usually with one of my parents beating on my bedroom door, take a shower so quick the water barely had time to hit the drain before I was done, find something Stacey or Raquita would flirt with me for wearing, and then burn my hands on multiple microwaved brown sugar Pop-Tarts while running to catch the bus.

The week I decided to join a gang, my morning routine went as it always had, except somebody—my pops—only left one Pop-Tart in the box, so your boy was a little hangry when he got on the bus. Which turned out to be unfortunate for Eric, the eighth-grade, bleach-blond-tips surfer bro on my bus ride. I'm good with surfers. Just not Eric. Eric annoyed everyone. His stop was just a few after mine and usually, if I planned what seat I was going to claim, I could dodge the hour-long Q&A session about what he didn't understand in a skit on the previous night's episode of *In Living Color*.

"Why does Wanda get mad if you touch her hair? And I don't understand why Homey doesn't play that?" (And you never will, Eric.)

Twenty minutes into our ride, Eric decided to move toward the back of the bus, where I was stewing in hunger-dom, and ask me, "Do all Black people—"

"Shut the fuck up" flew out of my mouth before I even realized I was saying it. I was too hungry to entertain Eric's desire for me to be a spokesman for the entire African Diaspora.

"Dude, calm down. I didn't even do anything," Eric said, smiling and throwing his hands up. I leapt on top of Eric from my seat across the aisle. I held him down and raised up my balled fist. Before I could get it all the way up for maximum punch efficiency, like King Hippo on *Mike Tyson's Punch-Out!!*, the bus jerked to a stop and our driver—in one of the rare moments he realized he had kids on the bus—yelled from the front, "Hey, hey, get back in your seats 'fore I kick y'all all off the goddamn bus and make ya walk!"

Like the scattering of roaches from the incandescent rays of lightbulbs, all the kids on the bus ran to their seats. I leapt off Eric and sat in my seat, eyes trained out the window.

"He's crazy. I mean, I didn't even do anything," Eric said to the people around us in a hushed whisper. It took every ounce of control to not let my 120-pound-when-soaking-wet body jump across the aisle again. In that moment, I decided I was going to figure out a way to get Eric to leave me alone for every bus ride in our shared future.

After about fifteen minutes of watching as the world outside the bus changed from the socioeconomic highs of South Tulsa to the socioeconomic lows of North Tulsa, we turned off Greenwood and pulled up in front of the school. As I crashed down the steps of the bus and left our driver sitting on his air-polluting throne, I spotted Jamar doing what Jamar did best.

Jamar—rest in peace—was one of those all bark/no bite kids who was always extra loud about how he was going to whoop your ass, like my drunk uncles playing spades, but he was sober and thirteen. He'd talk shit to anyone about anything, but when it came time to get down, he was David Copperfield.

That morning when I got off the bus, Jamar was ragging on an eighth-grader because his haircut was, as Jamar coined it, "fucked-up." Jamar was right, the kid's hair looked like his right-handed grandma got ahold of his head without her glasses and went to work with a pair of left-handed scissors. The eighth-grader didn't appreciate Jamar's loud-drunk-uncle-like tone and volume, so he called over one of his boys.

"Man, yo' momma so fat she use a VCR as a pager"—this escalated very quickly, but Jamar didn't back down from the two older kids and their jokes.

"Yeah but she gave it to yo' momma and I used it last night to beep her before I came over and hit that while you was sleeping. You can call me 'Step-daddy' if you want, son," Jamar said through a laugh.

No kid ever wants to hear some other kid say A) that their mom had relations with one of their classmates, or B) that they can call that classmate "Daddy." Jamar was ignited. He walked around school proclaiming he was going to fight not one but two eighth-graders after the bell rang. I knew I had to see this. Maybe there was something I could pick up from Jamar's fight that I could use on Eric. Jamar talked about fighting all the time. So he had to be able to back it up, right?

After the final bell rang, at 3:15 P.M. sharp, everyone bolted out of their seats and hauled ass toward the door. I got to the front steps of the school huffing and puffing like Omar Epps in *Juice*. The entire school was there.

"Where these fools at?"

"I can't miss my bus!"

"I'ma be late to practice but I don't even care."

"He gon' get his ass BEAT! Watch."

This was a highly anticipated school fight, more so than any of us had ever hoped for. Don King would have been proud—then he would have made us pay $49.99 to watch it. The two baby blue–wearing boys that Jamar was going to square off with were at the bottom of the steps waiting. "Man, this nigga ain't showing up. He—" But before he could finish his sentence someone yelled, "There he go!"

He'd come out at the far end of the building instead of the front. Jamar stood facing the crowd. "What's up then?" The two eighth-graders started walking in his direction and Jamar took off running—like he was, for real, Omar Epps in *Juice*. The boys took off after him—as did half of the people watching.

Jamar made it across Greenwood before he turned to taunt the boys. He humped the air: "I'm just going to y'all's mommas' houses real quick!" He didn't think the boys would

keep up their chase; Jamar was wrong. Tulsa produces athletes, some with God-like foot speed. The chase ensued and
the boys' internal turbo boosters kicked in. In a flash they
were on his heels.

Jamar lived across the street from school; he loved brag-
ging about how he didn't have to wake up early. So we knew
he was trying to get home before the boys could catch him,
but his plan didn't work. The boys caught up and squared off
in front of Jamar.

"Momma! Aye! Open the door!" Jamar started yelling.

"This bitch-ass calling his momma!" one of the boys said,
laughing, but sure enough, Jamar's mom answered the door.
With a hand-rolled cigarette masterfully balancing on her lip,
rollers in, and a bathrobe hanging off her shoulder, she yelled,
"Whatchu want?"

"They trying to jump me!" Jamar yelled back. She moved
her low-hanging eyes from Jamar to the boys, then back to
Jamar.

"Then you better not come in until you whoop they ass."
She sauntered inside and shut the door. The boys turned and
looked at each other, and then rushed Jamar. He in fact could
not back up all the shit-talking he always dished out. I felt
sorry for Jamar, sure, but I was transfixed by how these two
older dudes stuck together and had each other's backs.

DAY TWO

ANTWAN GRIFFIN WAS THE FRESH PRINCE OF NORTH TULSA. HE
was the best athlete in our school. He always had a fresh cut,
like a barber lived at his house. Gold earrings shined from his

ears like he robbed Mansa Musa's tomb, and he had every pair of Jordans. As a seventh-grader he had an eighth-grader girlfriend, somehow always had a Fresca from the teachers' lounge, and could throw up very intricate finger arrangements that represented his set. The rules of middle school awkwardness, acne, and voice-cracking didn't apply to him.

Everything Antwan wore had baby blue on it, and he rarely got caught in the same thing twice. It was like he went to the Eastland, Promenade, and Woodland Hills malls and bought every piece of baby blue clothing to hoard for himself.

Antwan also had deep connects with everyone in the school. If anything ever went down, someone always had his back. I don't remember him ever swinging on anyone, but I do remember a few different guys fighting *for* him, jumping in before he even had the chance to do it himself. Antwan had his own baby blue–wearing, gold chain–clanging Secret Service that would laugh at his jokes, fight for him if need be, and make sure he was always picked in pickup basketball. After watching what had happened to Jamar the previous day, I realized this was exactly what I needed to run up on Eric and stop his annoying and offensive line of questioning.

Samson and Elijah, the only kids I hung out with at school, weren't in a gang and had no intentions of ever being part of one. They both had hoop dreams, which I stumbled into a little later. Samson, skinny with a round head, a curious face, and Coke-bottle glasses, and Elijah, round body with fingernails that always needed a trim and a deep, booming voice, were born and raised in North Tulsa, and they knew all the nuances and intricacies of Black life in the city that I had only recently been calling home. By this point, Mikey wasn't around and I needed people to wade through the nonstop flow of geopolitical hood politics with. They were special counsel to my *Game of Thrones* middle school life.

Samson and Elijah didn't get caught up in middle school antics; they sat on the periphery watching it all go down. They were my perfect cheat code to integrating into the social dynamics of this new school, like my *Contra* Konami code: Up, Up, Down, Down, Left, Right, B, A. Which, like in the game, could literally mean the difference between life or death. One of the first crash courses they gave me was the lunchroom.

Our lunchroom was split into a few more groups than the usual: nerds, fly girls, athletes, art kids. Groups that the media told us were our only options. We had four additional groups that I didn't have at my previous school and weren't in any John Hughes movies. These groups dominated the landscape:

- Neighborhood Crips, who wore baby blue "Carolina blue kicks, fresh on the scene"
- Hoover Crips, who like their namesake and L.A. forefathers, wore a darker hue of blue
- Bloods, who wore red, often repping the Cincinnati Reds, which made no sense because the owner of the Reds at the time, Marge Schott, was a known and unapologetic racist
- Pirus, close cousins to the Bloods, who draped themselves in blood orange

The lunchroom Tetris that Samson and Elijah taught me to navigate was its own real-life video game; you had to skate around trouble while acknowledging the powers that be. It also made me realize I needed to align myself with the Neighborhoods.

"What do I have to do to become a Neighborhood?" I asked Samson and Elijah. They both looked at me. There was a brief pause followed by an outburst of laughter.

"He said . . . him . . . a Neighborhood!"

"What? Why y'all laughing? I'm serious."

Their laughter tapered off, and they both looked at me.

"I don't think you can," Elijah said.

"Are you stupid? You can't be in a gang!" Samson's bedside manner hadn't formed yet.

"Why not?" I asked, my face screwing up.

"Because you not a gang dude. They not gonna let you in and you wouldn't even look right in a gang," Samson said. I didn't have time to unpack his response; I was on a mission but I did down at my Jordache jeans and oversized polo.

"Whatever. You don't know," I said, walking away . . . but not too fast, because the lunchroom was hot and I still had to get to the other side without stepping on the wrong turf while tripping on my sagging bargain jeans.

—

LATER THAT DAY, I TOOK ADVANTAGE OF MY SCIENCE TEACHER'S alphabetical seat assignment and leaned over to the guy I knew could pull strings to get me in.

"Hey . . . hey, Antwan." Antwan turned toward me with a raised eyebrow. One of his gold and diamond earrings caught the sunlight, partially blinding me. With one eye closed, I went on, "Umm, so yeah, I was wondering . . . thinking . . . you know." Antwan didn't know; he gave me a deadpan stare. ". . . Can I . . . I wanna be like, you know . . ." A half smile spread across his face. "I mean I wanna be a Neighborhood." He looked at me, that half smile still on his face, partly like he was proud of me and partly showing something sinister, like he was going to enjoy the hell I was going to endure.

"I got you," he said.

DAY THREE

WHEN I GOT TO SCHOOL THE NEXT DAY, I RAN THROUGH THE hallways to the cafeteria trying to get a cinnamon bun— because there's nothing like public school sugar hidden in bleached GMO flour in the morning. On my way, I bumped into Antwan.

"Aye!" he yelled, the cafeteria doors just beyond him.

"What's up?" I said, slowing down, trying to play it cool while my nostrils sucked in the buttery smells of the cinnamon buns.

"Look, I talked to the homeys and you good. You can get in. Just gotta go through the . . ." Antwan's voice faded as the sweet smell of cinnamon and icing, the delicious fragrance of early-onset diabetes, wafted out of the cafeteria doors, distracting me. ". . . so when we got the numbers, we gon' do it, prolly in a couple days, aight?" I snapped my attention back to Antwan.

"Yeah. That's cool with me. I'm down for whatever," I replied, having no idea what he was talking about. The cafeteria doors closed and the bell rang.

—

HOURS LATER, I STOOD IN THE GYM, STOMACH ON EMPTY. "YOU stupid! You know you gotta trade your Supersonics Starter jacket for a jacket that got baby blue on it, right?" Samson said as we stood at the bottom of a rope in our skintight purple and white mandatory gym uniforms.

"What? Why? Na-huh. I can still keep my jacket," I replied as I looked up at the disc we had to touch as part of a physical fitness test.

"No. See this is why you not built for gangs. You don't get to choose. You in a gang, you do what they say."

I hadn't thought of it like that, but what did they know? "Y'all don't know. Y'all too scared to bang. So you don't know what I gotta do."

They both laughed. Elijah looked at me, then put his arm on my shoulder like he was Morgan Freeman in *Lean on Me*. "It's not too late to back out," he said. "You haven't been jumped in yet, so you can still change your mind and not go through with it."

"Man, bump y'all. I'm doing it. I already did it. I'm out."

I was so pissed that Samson and Elijah were trying to talk me out of joining the gang, that I glossed over a very important part: being "jumped in."

DAY FOUR

SECOND PERIOD THE NEXT DAY I LISTENED WHILE MR. CAMERON— who had a Colman Domingo deep, velvety voice and a past life as a stage actor in Chicago—instructed our science class on God knows what when Mercedes started toying with me. I couldn't stand Mercedes; she was in everyone's business and told everyone's business. My Burlington Coat Factory–brand denim hadn't even hit my seat before she said, "You know you gotta get jumped in tomorrow?"

A few kids turned their heads at the mention of a fight. My school got more hyped for fights than Bulls fans after winning three consecutive championships. I didn't even raise my eyes to meet Mercedes's when I replied, "Jumped in what?"

I could feel the class take a collective gasp as everyone clutched their imaginary gold chains.

"You don't know?" I didn't reply but looked up as she continued, "You gotta get jumped in the Neighborhoods. That's the last step."

What in the hell is this girl talking about?

"Jumped in? By who?" Between puberty and my nerves, my voice cracked, betraying the cool I was trying so hard to play. A huge smile wiped across Mercedes's face.

"Everybody in the 'Hoods. They all do it together." A few of the other bloodthirsty kids nodded their heads in excitement for the upcoming Colosseum-like event.

"Wha— How do you—"

A yardstick slammed against a table three times. Mr. Cameron—looking as regal as Sidney Poitier on the Oscars red carpet—stood at the front of the class holding a tiny pale piglet in his blue latex glove–covered hand. "I'm the booger with the sugar up in here, so y'all need to shut it and pay attention." Everyone in the room turned their attention forward as I sunk further into my chair.

I spent the entire fifty-minute class staring at the poor innocent dissected piglet, and thinking about my own inevitable fate. Where was Mikey? I needed him. He could explain this. He could help me get out of this. This was a major life moment I was staggering my way through, in desperate need of his sage advice on how to dodge slaughter.

It had been at least a year, maybe two, since I'd heard him. As I got older and Mikey appeared less and less, I usually referred to past advice—*Put your head down and keep it moving. It'll be alright*—but I felt lost at this moment. I was clinging, sure I couldn't get through this, not alive at least.

"We told you, you wasn't built for no gang," Samson proclaimed, waving a chicken finger in the air as we sat in the cafeteria for lunch. He dipped the chicken finger into a small container of nacho cheese. "You gotta fight back, so they know if something goes down you not scared and can hold your own and have they back too."

"And if you don't fight back, they just whoop yo' ass," Elijah, having Samson's back, added. I couldn't tell which they enjoyed more, the synthetically orange-colored canola oil cheese or watching the agony they were putting me through.

"How bad is it, for real?" I asked.

"It depends how many of them there are," Elijah said, gulping down grape soda. "Sometimes it's two or three and sometimes it's like eight."

"EIGHT!" I blurted out. If everyone in the cafeteria wasn't already looking at me and snickering, they definitely were now.

"Calm down, fool. Stop yelling," Samson said, leaning toward me over his lunch tray. "Just go ask Antwan how many of 'em it's gon' be, so you know." *Not a bad idea*, I thought. I looked over to Antwan's table, where just a few boys were eating lunch and laughing.

"I'll be back." I cha-cha slid through the cafeteria to avoid strolling into any hostile territory. I could feel everyone's eyes laser in on me. My skin prickled. My hearing, much like Nana's, became superhuman.

"That's him."

"He 'bout to get his ass mollywhopped!"

"He not even gon' make it out the hospital."

As I got closer and closer to Antwan's table, the realization set in that it didn't matter if I knew the number of my attackers or not. I was not trying to get jumped!

At the table sat Antwan and four of my would-be . . . Gang brothers? Gang associates? Gang comrades? Fellow gangstas?

"What up, Dub?" Antwan asked.

"Uh, oh, what's good, Ant?" I said and his brow furrowed at *Ant*. "Ant-wan. I mean Antwan." The floodgates under my arms opened and sweat started to soak into my shirt. He didn't say anything, so I continued, "Yeah, so I, um, heard that I'm supposed to get jumped in tomorrow?" Antwan and the group just stared; not one muscle on any of their faces moved. No answer—cool. I leaned a little closer to Antwan.

"What are you doing?" he asked, leaning his head back with a screwed-up face.

My eyes quickly glanced at the other boys at the table. "So is it going to be a bunch of y'all tomorrow?" I whispered. "Or just like—"

He cut me off with a smile. "Yeah, but it'll only be like six of us. You'll be good."

"Six! Great! Cool. Cool. Cool. Looking forward to the ceremony—I mean the jumping in of the gaaaa—" Our vice principal walked by, so I stopped short. "See you guys tomorrow then. Later!" I threw up a peace sign as I walked away.

"Did he just peace out?" I heard Tracey Williams say as I walked back to Samson and Elijah, who were waiting with bated breath. I plopped down at the table knowing that the end was near.

"What happened?"

"What he say?"

"It's happening tomorrow."

DAY FIVE

In the morning when I picked out my clothes, I asked myself what pieces of clothing had baby blue on them. Did any of said pieces provide extra padding? What did I want my parents to see me wearing when they came to the hospital? And did I have any underwear that wasn't white? Just in case.

Waiting for the bus, I questioned every decision I'd made the last five days. *Why? What was I thinking? Who actually wants to get jumped into a gang?* On the bus ride to school, I was reminded of why I was on this kamikaze mission in the first place: surfer bro Eric.

Eric waited for the bus inside the wrought-iron and goldleaf gates of his affluent neighborhood.

"Ugh," Tinisha said, "we're at Eric's stop."

Everyone on the bus responded.

"Here we go."

"Why we always gotta wait on him to come out of the gate? Just wait on the other side. Duh!"

"Somebody should kidnap him just so his parents see that them gates don't do nothing."

Eric surfed his way down the aisle and sat in the row just in front of mine. I was in my own world, thinking about the twelve fists of fury that would soon be crushing my ribs. After a few stops, he popped his head over the back of the seat and looked at me.

"Leave me alone, man. I don't have time to—"

Eric cut me off and with the intensity of a cult leader about to tell his congregation to drink the Kool-Aid; he very quietly said, "I just wanted to say, I'm sorry."

"What?"

"I think our fight was my fault and I just wanted to say that after thinking about it all week, I'm sorry."

"Whatever, man," I scoffed and looked out the window. Eric turned back around for all of fifteen seconds before he responded again.

"Um, also I just—I know you're in a gang now and well—I . . . I just want to make sure we're good because— you know . . ." He trailed off.

"I know what?" I asked. He did a quick look to make sure no one was listening.

"I don't want to get beat up by your homeboys." And there it was. He was apologizing because he thought I was going to get my goons on him. He was right! I was. But more importantly for me, it worked. Just the affiliation got him off my back.

We pulled up to school twenty minutes late. Luckily, I dodged a before-school ass-whooping but spent the rest of my day double taking my own shadow. Between classes, I went in and out of the hallways as fast as humanly possible. At lunch, I sat with my back to a wall facing the door so I could see who was coming in and out—mafia rules. In gym I lied and said I forgot my gym clothes at home, so I wouldn't get caught slipping in the locker room. By the time last period came around, I had found a way to circumvent every in-school scenario—a few of my classmates were even impressed.

Tracey looked at me like I was a new man. "They ain't got you yet?" she asked.

"Nope," I said, a sly grin plastered on my face.

"Hmm. Look at you. Maybe they not going to then. They didn't jump Antwan in."

I didn't even know that was a possibility. I exhaled a little. Maybe that was it. Maybe they knew I wanted to be in and that's all that mattered. Plus, I wasn't deadweight. They knew about how I almost gave Eric the business on the bus that Monday morning. When the last bell rang, instead of running through the halls to my locker, I floated like I was on a chariot circling around the Colosseum for my people to see me, Maximus Ellis, Emperor of all the Neighborhoods.

Midway through my noble glide to the front doors of the school, I saw Antwan.

"What up, 'hood?" he said.

"You know. Just chilling, mane," I responded.

"Tomorrow night we all linking up at the homey A.J. house, you should come through. Just hit me on the side-kick," he said. I had no idea how I was going to get my parents to take me across town to kick it on a Saturday night—also, he had a sidekick in seventh grade???

Regardless, I looked at him confidently and said, "Bet. I'll be there."

I exited through the front doors, toward the lined-up buses. The whole school was out and a few kids looked in my direction whispering; a few even smiled. *I made it*, I thought. The sun hit my face and I closed my eyes to enjoy it. The rays from the sun danced across my face. As soon as I opened my eyes, A.J.'s fist butted into my dance with the sun. Then Antwan's. Then Rodney's. Then Junior's. Then Keith's. Then Juwan's.

"Oh shit, it's going down," I heard someone yell. I popped up from the ground, not knowing which way was left or right, but I remembered one thing Samson and Elijah had said: "Fight back."

I started swinging. The only reason I know I connected a few punches is because my knuckles and wrist hurt like hell for the following few days. I kept swinging and swinging and occasionally landed a hit, but me fighting back only pissed them off and made them fight harder. Fight-or-flight took over. They surrounded me and I couldn't execute flight. I went into fight mode . . . for a little while.

I ended up on the ground, which is how most "jumping in of the gangs" go. The boys stood over me, blocking out daylight, as they continued punching and kicking. I had the taste of metal in my mouth, blood from my lip. I swear I heard "Make 'em say 'Ughhh, nah nah nah nah,'" as I absorbed blows. The school security guard, who I think may have been in on it, judging by how long it took him to get involved, started blowing his whistle and the boys ran off. I lay on my back, wincing in pain, and looked up at the sun through my quickly swelling eyelids. The rays stung, but I fought back and I got through it.

Samson leaned his head in over my face, blocking the sun. "You just got knocked the fuck out!" he screamed à la Smokey in *Friday*. A few people laughed as Elijah reached out a hand and helped me up to my feet.

"You alive?" he asked.

I nodded. "I think so."

"Guess you a Neighborhood then," he said.

The security guard approached. "What happened? Did those boys jump you?"

I looked at him through my good eye and I lied, "Nah, I tripped and they helped me up." He looked at me suspiciously. He knew I was lying but there wasn't much he could do unless I told on them, and as Mikey would say, "Snitches get stitches."

I slowly limped my way to the bus. I walked down the aisle, found an empty seat, and dropped into it. A smile spread across my face. The next thing I remember is the bus driver yelling, "Aye! Aye! Last stop. You gotta get off, Ali." I threw my backpack over my shoulder, hobbled down the stairs, and walked off like a champ.

DAY SIX

I'm not sure if Mikey would have been proud, but I was. I fought back and I didn't give up. The next morning was a Saturday and I woke up hungry. The night before, I'd gone straight into my room and passed out. My stomach may have woken me up, but it wasn't long before the real pain started to kick in. I had a pounding headache, sore ribs, and I could still taste metal in my mouth. I cleaned myself up as best I could and tried as hard as I could not to limp by clenching my butt cheeks as I walked into the kitchen, the pain radiating through my whole body.

My parents always started their Saturday morning singing and dancing their way through my dad's record collection. While they were remembering "what it was like in September," they cooked breakfast—the smell of bacon and chili omelets hit my nose. My parents were in their own world, so they hardly noticed anything was off until I winced from the spicy chili hitting my lip.

"What happened to your lip?" my mom asked.

I blinked rapid-fire. *Uh, lemme see. Well, I got in a fight with a kid named Eric on the bus Monday and then decided that I needed to join a gang so nobody would mess with me. I spent the week interviewing the candidates and reviewing my choices and after serious consideration, I was jumped into the Neighborhood Crips yesterday after school,* is what I wanted to say, but instead I said, "I got elbowed playing flag football in gym class." Real G's move in silence. Biggie said what he said.

"Isn't the whole point of the flag so y'all don't have to touch each other?" my mom asked.

"Accidents happen. That's the beauty of the game," my dad, a former football player, piped in from another room.

She rolled her eyes. "Hmm, well then I don't want him playing flag football." I waited for a few more of their favorite old-school jams to play, just to make sure the flag football thing had left my mom's mind, and then asked, "Can you take me to one of my friends from school house tonight?"

My mom, who missed her calling as a detective, stayed ready for an interrogation. "What friends?"

"My friends from school."

She sucked her teeth, "Your son in here trying to get smart!" she yelled over her shoulder in my dad's direction.

"What he want now?"

She looked over her shoulder, "Talkin' 'bout he wants to go to some 'friends from school house' to hang out tonight."

"What friends?"

"He not saying."

They do know I'm right here, right?

"Y'all know I'm right here?" I asked.

My mom looked up over her glasses: "Mmmhmmp."

I knew I couldn't push it. If this was going to work, I had to get my dad one-on-one and ask him to take me. I learned that one from Mikey: *Play them against each other and if Pops says yes first, then Moms will be cool with it.*

A FEW HOURS LATER, I WAS OUTSIDE ON THE ROOF HELPING MY dad clean leaves out of the gutters when I decided to take my shot. I figured enough time had passed for him to forget me asking my mom.

"Hey, um, later after we finished can you take me out North?" I asked.

My dad, lying on the roof, scraped his hand against the metal gutter, pulling out a jackpot of leaves. "What you going out there for?"

I had been thinking about this answer all day. I had the perfect response teed up.

"Just going to my friends from school house." I told y'all teenage boys are dumb.

"I guess—" but he couldn't finish his sentence because my mom, much like Nana—her mother—had superhuman hearing.

"Is he still asking about going to his 'friends from school house'?"

My dad looked up from the gutter. "You already asked your mom?"

"No," I lied.

"Well then how does she know about it?"

"I dunno." I shrugged my shoulders. He turned back to the gutter and didn't say anything. That was a "no."

By night, they hadn't budged. I was home moping, pissed I couldn't go hang out with my 'hoods . . . goons? . . . posse? . . . I still don't know . . . while the boys were just getting their night started. Fred, Antwan, and a few other guys all got together at A.J.'s house and the boys used it as an opportunity to do some initiation work. Fred was still new, and they said he had to prove he was down. After an hour or so, one of the boys pulled out his dad's gun and told Fred that the two of them had to play Russian roulette as his last step for initiation. Apparently a few of the other guys were apprehensive about it, and thought the kid who brought the gun was crazy, but after two rounds of nothing happening, he winked when one of them said, "I bet that shit ain't even loaded." They all laughed and then Fred squeezed the trigger, blowing a hole through his ear and out the opposite side of his head. He was fourteen years old.

DAY SEVEN

THE STORY MADE THE SUNDAY MORNING NEWS ON EVERY LOCAL
station. "Tulsa teen fatally wounded after a game of Russian
roulette in a gang initiation." A tiny picture of Fred flashed so
quickly onscreen that if you blinked, you missed it. My mom
turned the volume down on the TV.

"So sad. These boys out here playing gangbanger, trying
to be tough and they ending their lives before they even get a
chance to start 'em," she said as she moved to the kitchen,
where my dad was again making breakfast.

"Aye, come set the table," my dad called to me. I didn't
respond because even though the news had moved on from
the twelve seconds they gave Fred's story and tiny picture, I
hadn't. I was shook, in shock at the reality of it all.

"You hear me?" my dad yelled. "Come set the table!"

I snapped out of my fog. "Who?"

He peeked his head from around the corner. "You an
owl?" he said with a smile on his face—the perfect "Who,
who" dad joke. I tried as best as I could to pretend like all was
fine, but I was at a loss. My heart was racing, my body felt
numb. I knew Fred. We played basketball together. We sat
next to each other on a field trip to Bartlesville to see the only
hotel Frank Lloyd Wright ever designed. In the few mornings
I could get to school on time to make it to the cafeteria, Fred
consumed more chocolate milk than he did food. He was the
first "friend," or at least someone my age, of many, who I
knew, that I ever lost. I sat at the table in a daze, picking over
most of my food. A combination of not having an appetite
and feeling nauseous.

I lay in bed later not knowing what to do. *Do I just have a normal Sunday and watch football with my dad? Do I do my homework? Maybe I should call somebody from school and see if they know anything?* I wanted to do everything but couldn't do anything. Tears welled up in my eyes. I fought them because, well, I was a teenage boy and that's what we were told to do. I wasn't emotionally or mentally prepared, not that one should be, for having a friend fatally shoot himself.

I started thinking about my parents. They had no idea where I'd been asking to go the previous night, or who was going to be there. They didn't know that I'd made the impulsive decision to join a gang earlier that week. They had no idea that the kid who died went to the same school as me or, better yet, that he was in the same gang as me. They knew none of it, and in that moment I realized it'd be better if they never did.

I grabbed my *Space Jam*–themed Trapper Keeper from my backpack. I flipped through, in search of a sheet of paper with numbers scribbled on it. When I found it, I tore it out and tiptoed like the Pink Panther through the house to the phone that hung on the kitchen wall to the right of the garage door. Much like my aunt Shanice, I slipped into the far edge of the garage. I had the number. I had the phone. I had privacy. *Now what am I going to say???*

I couldn't figure out anything that didn't sound ridiculous. None of the conversation starters I ran through in my head felt like there was an awareness of the gravity and tragedy of the situation. So instead of trying to script what I was going to say, I just called. I paced back and forth while I listened to the phone ring. Once. Twice. Three times . . . *It's going to voice-mail,* I thought, but on the fourth ring, Antwan picked up.

"Hello?" he said, lifting his voice to make the word into a question.

"It's Dub. What's up?" I whispered, looking over my shoulder toward the garage door.

"Shit. Just got home from the police station. You lucky you ain't come last night." *You can say that again,* I thought.

"Anyway, what you—"

"I'm out!" I blurted, cutting him off.

The words hung there. There was a long beat of silence until Antwan said, "Yeah, I feel you. Me too."

As a friend, Mikey needed nothing from me in order to have my back. I never really needed a gang. I always had homeboys, even if I didn't realize it. Samson and Elijah looked out for me even when I wanted to send myself swinging into a gang. It didn't matter what color I wore, I didn't have to go through the agonizing inevitability of getting jumped to be boys with them. I just had to show up and be me. Unapologetically me.

ROAD TRIPPIN'

"I'm not getting jerked around today. Understand me?"

FOR SIX OR SEVEN AMAZING SUMMERS, I ROAD-TRIPPED WITH my paternal grandparents from Sacramento, California, down to Tampa, Florida, up to Washington, D.C., and then back across the country. Road trips for my family were less about vacations and more about avoiding the cost of flying. It was how we visited my great-great-grandma Choice; how I got dropped off and later picked up for my summers in Sacramento; and one of the ways we all spent time together.

My grandpa hated flying. He hated getting dressed up in his perfectly pressed brown Sunday suit and fat yellow tie, carrying a bag of fried chicken—which he'd eventually drop on his perfectly pressed brown Sunday suit—in one hand and a suitcase in the other.

Any chance Grandpa Booker got to get behind the wheel and control his own destiny, he did. And although he ran the minivan like Jerry Jones runs the Dallas Cowboys—calling all the shots, despite whatever the quarterback, captain, coach, and GM say—Booker also took my cousins and me to places, and through experiences, that we'll never forget.

From the deep rust-toned canyons of the Grand Canyon, to the Caribbean-blue waters of South Florida, to Martin Luther King Jr.'s Ebenezer Baptist Church in Atlanta and the site of the 16th Street Baptist Church bombing in Birmingham, Alabama, we saw every nook and cranny of the United States.

Mikey and I learned that you couldn't drive under the Gateway Arch in St. Louis. We had Rita's water ice in Philly and Giordano's deep dish in Chicago. We ate blue crabs for the first time in a split-level house in Virginia. The only crab we knew was Sebastian, and he was red. We saw it all, and my grandpa and grandma loved showing it to us.

Austin, TX, to Roswell, NM

"Let's go!" Big Dub yelled from the driver's seat of his gleaming maroon Mazda RX-7.

A few months earlier Mikey, my mom, and my nine-year-old self had slowly peeked our heads out of the finest metal window blinds that base housing had to offer and saw my dad sitting in a brand-new car that none of us recognized.

"What in the hell he do now?" my mom mumbled under her breath, as she cut her eyes like a samurai blade through the window. Mikey and I looked at each other and simultaneously mouthed, RACE CAR! Before we could move, my mom had already flown out the front door, leaving a trail of smoke behind her.

Before this point, we had always been a one-car household. My dad worked on the Air Force bases we lived on, so there wasn't a need for a second car. My mom was the primary driver of our early '80s white Ford Escort—a car my dad couldn't stand driving. So, unbeknownst to my mom, he went out one day and used the three nickels Uncle Sam gave him as a down payment on a maroon Mazda RX-7 two-seater with no back seat. There were three of us. Plus Mikey.

Once the dust settled on my dad's impulse purchase, my parents planned our first road trip in the new car: My dad and I would drive to Sacramento, where I would get dropped off to spend the summer with my grandparents.

When our departure day arrived, I busted through the door with my packed bags, headed straight to the race car's passenger side, but before I could reach the car door handle, my mom scooped me up. I tried to fight my way out of her extremely tight hug, but she was—and still is—too strong. It was like bear hugs were named after her. I gave in and dropped my frail arms to my sides. She kissed me on the forehead, tears forming in the corners of her eyes. "Don't be starting no trouble, and call me every week. Okay?"

"Okay," I said, exaggerating the *ay,* while wiping the kiss off my face. I jumped in and we took off rolling. Mikey, who was crammed in the back, popped his face between the heap of bags to wave goodbye to my mom as I hung out the window shouting "Bye!," never thinking about what three months of her only child being gone would be like for her.

The fresh smell of a real new car, not the spray at the car wash, drew my easily distracted attention to every detail in the car. I touched the stitching of the seats, the buttons on the stereo system, the tinted sunroof—it was like being in a space-ship.

I reached for the radio and my dad made one noise: "Ah." He didn't have to say any more; he was giving me "Don't you ever touch a Black man's radio" far before Chris Tucker improvised the line in *Rush Hour*. The radio was off-limits. Mikey leaned forward and said, "Fine, no radio, but maybe he'll let you drive?" My dad had let me sit in his lap and hold the steering wheel of the Escort while making circles in the grocery-store parking lot, waiting for my mom, so maybe Mikey was right.

"You gonna let me drive?" I asked my dad as we pulled onto the highway. With his eyes trained on the road, never looking away, he said, "We don't have time to be playing around." I sank in my seat a little. Mikey, realizing he'd set me up for disappointment, whispered, "That's . . . I mean he's right, we don't have a lot of time."

We left Austin for Sacramento at about 1:30 P.M. on a Friday afternoon and my dad had to be back to work, in Austin, at 6:00 A.M. the following Tuesday. It's a twenty-six-hour trip from Austin to Sacramento. That meant by the time we arrived in Sac, he'd only be there for eighteen to twenty hours before driving another twenty-six hours back to Austin—with about six hours of sleep before going to work Tuesday morning. Why didn't we fly? We were broke, and gas was only seventy to eighty cents a gallon back then.

Mikey and I spent the first few hours of the trip with our faces pancaked against the windows, staring at all the trucks that passed by. Every time one passed, we'd punch our fist in the air and then pull down like we were yanking on a rope, in an attempt to get the truck drivers to blow their horns. If we'd get a driver to oblige, we'd yell at the top of our lungs, "Unh-unnnnnnnnh!" trying to imitate the sound of the horn. We did this for what felt like the entire eternity it took just to get across the flat, never-ending, and geographically bankrupt landscape of West Texas. It took hours, but as soon as we crossed the state line into New Mexico, we were met with an enticing proposition.

Ahead of us were miles and miles of billboards advertising an extraterrestrial experience at the International UFO Museum and Research Center, as well as alien jerky. We were two hours from the alien capital of the world—Roswell, New Mexico—and Mikey and I *lit up* . . . for completely different reasons. I was hyped to see a real-life alien and eat whatever alien jerky was. Mikey, on the other hand, was afraid he was going to get abducted and taken to a galaxy far, far away where he'd have to be some green alien's imaginary friend.

100 MILES TO UFO'S

As we passed the sign on the side of the highway, I turned to Mikey excitedly, but he shook his head from side to side. His eyes screamed, *Do not ask him!* I noticed but was too hyped to consider his feelings. There was no way my dad would deprive his son from learning the truth about what was in space. He didn't stand for fuckery, but when fuckery and education met, if you could sell him on the educational benefits and it wasn't going to cost his whole check, he was all in.

"Can we stop to see the alien museum?" I asked. "My science teacher said there are billions of galaxies and in every one there's planets and aliens have to exist because it's crazy to think we're the only life forms out there."

He was silent for a beat. "Is that what she said?"

I nodded my head up and down so fast I could have gotten whiplash. The seed had been planted and now I had a hundred miles to get my dad on board.

SEE A REAL-LIFE ALIEN IN 70 MILES

"Soooo, I was thinking we could stop to see the aliens and then eat lunch. Maybe get alien jerky?" I said, and then, appealing to his practical side, I threw out, "And we can get gas for the rest of the trip, an all-in-one stop, so we won't have to stop again."

"What if there isn't a gas station near the museum?" my dad asked. There had to be a gas station there though, right? I mean, what did the aliens use to fuel their ships? I tried that, but my dad didn't say anything. Mikey leaned forward with a big grin on his face, "Ugh, too bad. We were so close, huh?"

At fifty miles from the museum the billboards started becoming more frequent.

I looked out the corner of my eye to see if my dad saw the sign.

"I saw it," he said without looking at me. "But we don't need to stop, we got plenty of gas."

FORTY MORE AND YOU'LL SEE A SPACESHIP SOAR

"My teacher said that aliens probably don't look anything like they make them on TV. She says they probably look just like us."

IN THIRTY MILES WE'LL SHOW YOU WHAT UNCLE SAM WON'T

"I wanna be a spaceship pilot one day."

"Join the Air Force, then."

"We can see the difference between the spaceship and the airplanes you work on."

Just before the twenty-miles-away billboard, it hit me. I had to pee. If I could hold it, I could tell my dad as we got closer it was an emergency, and he'd have to stop. And since we'd already be there, we might as well go to the museum and see if E.T.'s cousins were really in there.

At first I thought about the desert, but to think about the desert meant I was trying *not* to think about water, which made my mind wander back to water. My legs tightened.

Mikey leaned forward again. "It's hot, huh? You know what I could use? Some cold water. Or maybe swimming in a pool. Yeah, that would cool me off. How 'bout you?" my disloyal/backstabbing/afraid-of-aliens friend said. I glared at Mikey but my dad thought I was looking at him.

"What's your problem?" he asked.

"I have to pee!" I blurted out and as soon as I did, I knew there was no more waiting. I had to go and I had to go right then. "I think I'm gonna pee on myself. I can't hold it," I said. My dad grabbed a Pepsi Clear bottle from the cup holder (if you don't know Pepsi Clear, look it up). He pressed his knees under the bottom of the steering wheel to guide the car, and used both hands to screw the cap off, roll the window down, and pour out the leftover Pepsi Clear contents. When he finished, he took control of the wheel with his hands and handed me the empty bottle.

"Go in this," he said. I lifted the bottle to my eye like a

telescope. "I can't go in there. It won't fit." Eyes on the road, he said, "You just point in the bottle, not put it in." I had never peed in a bottle before. *Is that even a real thing?* I thought to myself. *Also, he just wasted some good Pepsi Clear!* I took the bottle from him and eyed the opening. Closer . . . closer . . . inspecting it. *What makes him think I could do this? How did he even come up with this? Was it something he just did on his own or did his dad teach him?* I looked between my dad, the bottle, and Mikey. Mikey gave me a *Don't look at me* face and said, "I never did that before so I'm no help, but it's gotta be better than peeing on yourself." He was right. Gingerly, I unzipped my jorts, pulled my underwear down, put the bottle between my legs, and let go, trying not to spray all over the car like a fire hose.

A few miles later, we sailed by the museum exit. I mashed my face against the glass and watched my chance of a lifetime slip out of my hands. I looked back at Mikey, who leaned against the tiny back seat with a look of relief on his face. He'd dodged a bullet. I didn't learn if aliens were real or if the government had a secret testing facility that day, but I did learn how to pee in a bottle while in a car, how to handle other drivers' road rage, and how to read a map. My dad's ability to both calmly and quickly problem-solve and improvise, on road trips and beyond, is still something I aspire to; whether my dad knew it or not, that moment laid the foundation for every road trip I've taken as an adult. During the rest of that trip, Mikey and I observed my dad take in the silence of the desert, sing along with the radio to stay awake, navigate highway closures, stop only when needed—for gas, to put air in the tires. His skills were matched only by those of my paternal grandparents, my grandma Barbara and my grandfather Booker, who had different approaches to putting problems to rest.

SACRAMENTO, CA, TO VENICE BEACH, CA

FOR THE LONGEST TIME I WAS TERRIFIED OF BIRDS. I WOULD CROSS the street before I crossed a bird's path. It started when one summer, after watching the wrong movie followed by asking the wrong question, I got chased by a demonic prehistoric bird, which gave me enough trauma and fear to hold on to for a long time.

Halfway through one of my summer stints in Sac, when I'd spent the first half begging to go to Disneyland, my grandma decided we'd take a road trip down to Southern California. My dad's middle brother, my uncle Don, had just begun working for American Airlines and was based in Long Beach, California. My grandma Barbara, who is the jet-setter in our family, loved the fact that she now had unlimited free flights and a free place to stay in Long Beach.

The road trip itself was like the center of California: not very memorable. The only notable moments were seeing a goat on the edge of a mountain as we hit a stretch of I-5 called the grapevine and my grandfather Booker yelling that we had to turn the AC off and turn the heat on or the car would over-heat and explode. (I don't know if there is real science to Booker's car-cooling technique, but from my first car to my current car, I turn on the heat, usually in the middle of the summer, anytime my engine temperature needle moves a fraction.)

The night before we left Sacramento for Long Beach, Mikey talked me into staying up late to watch TV because my parents never let me stay up late, even in the summer—late to them was past 7:00 P.M. At this time, I was the only grandkid on this side of the family, so my grandparents let me do anything I wanted. Mikey figured they had to spoil me. "Might as well get as much in while we can." I couldn't argue, so we spread out on the couch. My grandparents had all the cable channels; Grandpa Booker insisted on being able to "watch whatever I want whenever I want, 'cause that's what I work for." But at night, the only thing that was on was infomercials.

The first thing we saw, as the TV slowly blinked on, was "The Potty Putter!" The large graphic splashed across the screen. The global stardom of Tiger Woods hadn't come along yet, so Black people playing golf already seemed crazy, but Black people sitting on the toilet while playing golf . . . Nah! Next.

Susan Powter popped up onscreen, with a look of a deep intensity that made it feel like she was staring through the camera, over the airways, past your TV screen, and into your soul. "STOP THE INSANITY!" she screamed. Mikey yelped and snatched the remote, fumbling around until he changed the channel.

"Alright, now I'm real fast, lemme tell you what I think and this will come to pass, my name is Geek, I put 'em on as a shocker, man I love these BluBlockers . . ."

Dr. Geek filled the small screen, rocking a sombrero on the Venice Beach boardwalk while wearing the cult-favorite sunglasses, BluBlockers. Instantly, Mikey and I were enthralled. He was rapping, and wearing a pair of sunglasses that not only blocked the sun, but the brown reflective lenses revealed the world of Venice, California, around him back at us. We were sucked in.

As the infomercial went on, Dr. Geek flipped his rapping style and imitated Muhammad Ali for a few bars—"I float like a butterfly, sting like a bee, yep the Blockers okay with me"—before switching it up again to sound like a Bugsy Siegel caricature: "Yeah see it's a face, these Blockers they go with my hat." We were so engrossed that before we even noticed, the genius commercial programming gods rolled right into another infomercial.

And there she was, sitting at a radio desk with headphones hugging her head wrap and a silver microphone just to the side of her mouth, a regal and charismatic woman who could change our lives. Our good friend, Miss Cleo the psychic, for ninety-nine cents a minute would take your call with her nondescript Caribbean accent—her accent slipped in and out of different islands like a ship in and out of ports—and flip some tarot cards over and read your future. Or just read you. Although she was talking to a caller onscreen, Mikey felt like Miss Cleo was calling him out: "Stop the foolishness and grow up!" she barked. Mikey's ears perked up because we had just gotten yelled at by Grandpa to stop playing and go to bed. Luckily he had a superpower for passing out as soon as he got horizontal. So we could stay up. After Miss Cleo read Mikey, he couldn't get out of his feelings, so we flipped a few more channels until an old-timey black-and-white movie came onscreen. Alfred Hitchcock's *The Birds*.

A blond woman walks across a crosswalk through a very clean San Francisco street. After a way-too-young-to-be-whistling-at-a-grown-woman kid catches her attention, she stops, smiles at the future predator's objectification, and then looks to the sky to see a whole gang of blackbirds swarming overhead. The woman then turns and walks into a pet store.

She buys two birds, and as the movie progresses, a seagull swoops at her head, a bird hits a window and falls to its death. We had no clue what any of this, collectively, meant; and we had no idea what was about to go down.

Somewhere between the children being attacked as they ran for their lives from the school building and Tippi Hedren being trapped inside a phone booth, Mikey and I slowly realized that we were too far gone to turn back.

Mikey dove behind couch pillows. I grabbed the leftover cushions Mikey hadn't used and frantically covered myself, leaving just enough of a gap to continue fear-watching. As the birds began upping their rats-with-wings assault, my chest pumped up and down with the pressure of an oil derrick. After about forty minutes of hyperventilating and choking on the fumes of my own bad breath, the horror of Bodega Bay finally ended. Roy and Tippi run out of town as thousands of birds glide over their newly claimed territory.

Mikey and I sat still for a beat, slowly removing our pillow shields. As the credits rolled and we kicked off the TV, a new realization set in. We had to walk down the long—really not that long—hallway to our bed. Mikey carried a single pillow against his chest like armor for the treacherous journey. I followed close behind. We padded our way through my grandparents' mid-century one-story house—every shadow sending us into a spiral—until we finally arrived at the bedroom. My uncle's old bedroom. Mikey and I cautiously craned our necks around the door, checking to make sure no birds clawed their way into the room. The bright moon made a few of my uncle

Don's dance trophies cast deep shadows on the wall, which looked to almost be swaying.

"Throw something at them," Mikey said in the slightest of whispers. I gingerly took off one of my socks and heaved it toward the trophies like a shot-putter at the Olympics. In a flash we closed the door and listened. Nothing. Mikey and I scrambled to the bed, diving under the covers. There may not have been a demonic bird in the room, but we weren't jinxing it. The head of the bed was under the window that led out toward the driveway. Mikey insisted that if there was a late-night ambush, we needed to be able to see it coming. So we laid our heads at the foot of the bed and stared at the window all night long.

The next morning, dry-eyed from sleep deprivation and terrified to get out of bed, Mikey and I lay frozen until my grandfather barged through the door yelling, "Wash ya butt and brush ya teeth. I wanna be on the road in the next hour." He was not a man full of morning platitudes but rather a man of direct action.

My toes gripped the shag-rug bath mat as I ran a rag under warm water and then reached under my shirt with a wash-cloth to wipe my armpits. After my "bath" I headed into the kitchen, where usually my grandmother would have been up for hours waiting for her one and only grandchild with eggs and bacon frying on the stove.

When Mikey and I got there, there were no eggs, no sizzling bacon, no Minute Maid frozen concentrated orange juice, no Grandma. My grandpa walked by the kitchen and saw me standing there like a stunned soldier and barked, "Get you something to eat out the freezer in the back," as he stomped past the kitchen door. "Your grandma is outside packing the car." *Venice, here we come,* I thought I heard her say.

I don't know if this is a generational thing or a scarcity thing, but grandparents and deep freezers go together like Wilford Brimley and Liberty Medical "diabetuhs" commercials between episodes of *All My Children* and *One Life to Live.* And Booker's deep freezer is where I was sent to find my breakfast.

Twenty Lean Cuisines, three bags of ham hocks, one cow tongue, hella Jimmy Dean sausages, a couple Pillsbury Doughboy cinnamon roll tubes, and a partially frostbitten hand later, I found two boxes of Great Starts scrambled eggs, homestyle potatoes, and bacon for Mikey and me. We inhaled the watery microwaved eggs and flimsy, undercooked bacon right as Booker walked in and grumbled, "Time to hit the road, Jack." Mikey and I weren't sure why he was calling us Jack, but we weren't questioning a career military man.

THE TRIP DOWN THE GOLDEN STATE WAS UNEVENTFUL; THERE was little outside our windows or inside the car to keep Mikey and me entertained—except for an emergency bathroom stop from our stomachs doing the Kid 'n Play dance (funny thing about those Great Starts breakfast, they start great but they don't tell you about the ending). Hours later, as soon as we got to my uncle Don's apartment in Long Beach, Mikey and I begged to see Venice Beach. We had told my grandpa all about the Geek and how we wanted to see what he had and maybe catch a glimpse of Arnold Schwarzenegger lifting weights at Muscle Beach. Booker said he wasn't "interested in none of that." Luckily, my uncle and grandma agreed with me. We couldn't just sit in his apartment. Book decided to stay at Uncle Don's and we headed out on an adventure.

The first thing we saw were Rollerbladers, skateboarders, street performers, and vendors selling everything from cotton candy to churros. Venice Beach was everything Mikey and I had seen on TV. We sprinted as fast as we could through the soft granular sand to the shoreline. Our first few steps were filled with youthful ignorance—until walking began to feel like a chore. We didn't realize that our shoes would fill with sand and that we'd sink with every step we took, slowing us down. I lifted my right foot, trying to take off my shoe while standing, and hopped around on one leg like I was Vanessa Bell Calloway in *Coming to America*. Shoes off.

Now barefoot, we started to run again, and within seconds the hot sand began burning our feet. This is why gangsters don't wear sandals. Got it. Mikey and I high-kneed our way across the sand like HBCU drum majors, and every step we took was immediately followed by an "Ouch," "Ahhhh," or "Ha, haw, hawt, hawt, hawt." It felt like walking across fire. We ran into the murky blue-brown water, cooling our feet, until my grandma and uncle called us over to the towel they had spread out.

Mikey and I plopped down and began digging for snacks. I popped a can of Pringles while Grandma opened a ziplock bag of cherries—they were out of season but you can get anything year-round in California—and my uncle started going in on a Ralphs sandwich. Within minutes we were surrounded and being squawked at to give up our food. Seagulls.

They swooped in from the nearby lifeguard tower, also known in my adolescent mind as the *Baywatch* tower. The birds circled over our blanket and landed nearby. "Grandma, why are the birds pecking their necks?" I asked, watching one land, its neck constantly jutting forward as it moved quickly in a zagging line toward me. She leaned in with a big smile on her face, and said, "So they can peck your brains."

"Aww, hell nah!" Mikey yelled. "Man, they got her too. She's in on it. We gotta go!" I froze and then . . . I spiraled: *Don't she know this ain't a game? It's real out here. I quit school because of recess! Is this why she brought me here? She kept saying over and over how she wanted to take me to the beach. And she knew I was up late watching TV. She had to have known there was nothing else on but* The Birds. *Is this because I spilled Kool-Aid on her couch?*

I couldn't sit there and become the Tippi Hedren of Venice Beach. Mikey and I had to get off that beach. My breath started to pick up like I had just chased the ice cream truck, barely catching it before it turned the corner. The top of my nose was dewy from anxiety sweat. My stomach started to gurgle like my lactose-intolerant body had drunk a gallon of milk. I kept replaying scenes from *The Birds* over and over in my head, birds diving for Tippi. It was a never-ending *SportsCenter* segment of the same dunk over and over, but instead Stuart Scott was using his witty wordplay to call this bird attack. The seagulls hopped closer, sensing food and fear.

"We gotta go!" Mikey belted out. "If we stay here, this ain't gon' end well and I don't want this to be the end. Not like this."

"Grandma, can we go?" I quickly asked. The smile on her face dropped.

"Go? Boy, we just got here," she said. "What you talkin' 'bout go?"

By this point, my breathing was out of my control; my

chest heaved. My body felt fully out of my control and I was fully crippled by fear. I looked at my grandma.

"If we stay on the beach, the birds are gonna peck my brains out and eat me like they did the woman in the movie," I said. Moisture collecting to tears that started congregating together in the corners of my eyes.

"Aww, baby," she said, softening, "I was just joking. Grams didn't mean it. Come here," and she pulled me into her arms. The tears had gathered into big drops of salt water. I still couldn't get my labored breathing steady until she and my uncle moved us farther down the shore and made sure to help shield me from the vultures—seagulls—and anytime one came too close, she didn't let me run. She held me still and together we shooed them away. She made me realize that if I faced them, then I'd be okay.

MOHAVE, CA;
GRAND CANYON NATIONAL PARK, AZ;
ALBUQUERQUE, NM;
AMARILLO, TX;
TULSA, OK

MY LAST ROAD TRIP WITH MY GRANDPARENTS WAS TO THE GRAND Canyon. Sometime during the year before the trip, Grandpa talked Grandma into buying a new van, since they were now taking care of my two younger cousins full-time. Grandma bought a Toyota Previa, which looked like it came from the future. It was sloped in the front and rounded in the back in a way that no other minivan on the market was. The front windshield was massive; you could see the entire road ahead of you. Inside, the front console looked like something out of *Star Wars*. The contoured curves created an upside-down W shape that allowed for Grandpa's long legs to stretch out without hitting anything. In the back it had two separate captain's chairs and a third-row bench. The air-conditioning system was frigidly pristine, and the state-of-the-art sound system came with a CD player and speakers spread throughout the cabin. It was the *perfect* vehicle for a family road trip.

By the time I arrived in Sacramento for the summer, my grandpa had maps spread all over the dining table. Grandma said he had been studying the maps for weeks. There was no Google Maps back then, and this was years before TomTom. Almost every day, Grandpa would study those maps like he was me cramming for a pop quiz. By the end of the summer he had memorized every highway, side road, freeway, and interstate from California to Maine. Grandpa decided, with his extensive knowledge of the American infrastructure system, that we were going to leave Sac early and road-trip back to Oklahoma. This was Grandpa's first opportunity to get the Previa out on the open road, and he thought it'd be good for my cousins, Katrina and Rashawn, at five years old and three years old, to "see the country they live in."

WE HIT THE ROAD IN THE SWELTERING MAKE-YOUR-UPPER-LIP-sweat heat of late July. As we started backing out of the driveway I had the back row all to myself—my personal Previa paradise. My cousins sat just in front of me in the captain's chairs. I really tried to have an open line of communication with them and explain where the boundaries of their space ended and mine began. But very quickly into the trip it was clear that my messaging needed work, because they were in my space before the Previa could hit the highway.

Before we reached the Sacramento city limits, Grandpa barked that he had two stops he wanted to make: the airplane graveyard in Southern California, and Grand Canyon National Park in Arizona. He made it as clear as water melted from an Alaskan glacier when we left that these were the *only* sights we would be seeing on the trip. Any other detours would take him too far off the meticulously mapped-out route he had in his head. And he wasn't having that. If you asked to stop he would first frown, which would turn into a barely audible low growl before he spent an hour filibustering all the reasons he wasn't going to make a stop.

We drove down the center of the state on CA 99. It was one of those days that was so hot that you could see rays of heat dancing as they rose off the asphalt, but that didn't stop Booker from trying to hold off putting the air-conditioning on. Booker was on a mission; the fuel range on the Previa was 423 miles, and he wanted to push the car to 420-ish miles on a single tank of gas. His plan was to drive from Sac nonstop for 350 miles, until we got to Mojave to see the airplane graveyard, also known by its actual name, Mojave Commercial Airliner Storage. Needless to say, Book's plan to drive five hours with no AC and no stops—with two kids under six, a twelve-year-old, and my grandma in the car—hit a few bumps.

We stopped at a truck stop: "Grandpa, I gotta peepee," Katrina yelled about thirty-five minutes into the trip. We had barely just left the Sacramento city limits. Book's face scrunched into a scowl. Ten minutes later, Mikey and I were flipping through tabloids, catching up on my role models—Oprah and aliens—while Katrina peed. After the bathroom break and snack-grabbing, we got back to the car and Booker announced, "We ain't gon' be stopping every five minutes."

We stopped at a Subway: "I think I need to go again," Katrina said. "You thank or you know?" he grumbled. "I know I need to go again," she said. Booker pulled off at the next exit.

We stopped on the side of the road: "I'm 'bout to go on myself!" Katrina yelled as she ran from my cordoned-off safe haven in the back of the van, which she had breached, to the front. Grandpa yanked the Previa to the shoulder of the road. He stood in front of her to hide her from passing cars, and gave her Rashawn's baby wipes when she finished.

We stopped at McDonald's: "McDonald's! Can we stop?" Katrina asked Grandpa as she leaned between the two front seats. "No. Y'all already ate," Book barked. "But I gotta use it again," said Katrina. "Me too, me too" said Rashawn. His language skills hadn't kicked in well enough for him to form sentences yet, but he knew how to repeat very well. Grandpa pulled off a few exits down the road. There was no ball pit but we did get Happy Meals.

Seven-and-some-change hours later, we finally made it to the airplane graveyard in Mojave. It was the coolest and creepiest thing Mikey and I had ever seen. Grandpa drove us up a nearby hill where you could look down into the graveyard with no obstructions. There must have been thirty or forty planes holding space there.

Mikey and I imagined finding pilots still in their seats, ready for takeoff. For the few older prop planes, Mikey could spin the propeller and I'd steer us into flight. Or maybe we'd find treasure—treasure we'd spend on cool things like an A-Team lunch box and a new Huffy bike.

"These airplanes are old, Grandpa. They don't even work. Can we go?" Katrina said, breaking Mikey and me out of our flying daydream. After a few minutes, we loaded back in the car and took off down the highway. Booker's mood was lighter. There may have been more detours than he expected, but he had accomplished the day's mission.

The next day, after sleeping in a motel that had surely seen more bodies than the Mojave coroner's office, Grandma and Grandpa wrangled us into the car to head to our next stop. Grand Canyon National Park was supposed to be just a seven-hour drive from Mojave, and after the previous day's trip, Grandpa was not in the mood to play the stop-every-hour game with Katrina. As we loaded into the car, he made it very clear to everyone: "I'm only stopping at planned stops. Wear a diaper if you need to pee. I'm not getting jerked around today. Understand?"

Grams looked at him from the passenger seat. *Who you talking to? I know you ain't talking to me* was the expression spread across her face.

"I was talking to the kids. Not you," he said in a whisper, tone changed, thinking we wouldn't hear him in the back. Book didn't want to catch Grandma's smoke. Mikey and I smiled at each other. The Previa pulled out of the motel-of-murders parking lot and we headed east on I-40.

We did make it to Grand Canyon National Park that day—albeit there were some unplanned stops, like to a McDonald's built like a vintage train car in Barstow—but when we pulled in past the burnt-orange sign at the edge of the park, Grandpa smiled. He'd finally made it. He took us out on the rocks, and we stood in silence as we took in the views. The red rock canyon carved with deep lines, like layers of red velvet cake, went as far as our eyes could see. Grandpa sighed. He was at peace.

In some of the canyon walls, we saw old dwellings built by the Hopis, and Grandpa told us that they had lived in this area for hundreds of years before colonization. I remember thinking how small I felt. Mikey was afraid of heights, so he didn't get close to the edge, but even through his fear, he was in awe of what was in front of us. As the sun began to set, our section of the canyon was covered in a golden glow that made the whole place seem that much more magical. Mikey and I stood in the glow while the cousins ran around behind us. Grandma leaned on Book's shoulder, and we watched the sun dip into the horizon.

WHAT WAS SUPPOSED TO BE A TWO-DAY TRIP BECAME THREE, BUT Grandpa had made it to the two things he wanted to show us. He was a little carefree the next day as he drove us through three more Native reservations—the Zuni, the Navajo, and the Pueblo. With each one he told us about how Native folk were pushed onto reservations by the government, and how they were the true shepherds of the West.

We stopped for gas just below the giant brown and rust-red rocks of the Sandia Mountains in Albuquerque, New Mexico. Passing through Amarillo, Texas, we saw giant graffiti-tagged Cadillac cars flipped over and half-buried in the khaki desert floor. We smelled at least a million cows as the Previa jetted through the panhandle of Oklahoma, before we finally pulled into our last stop of the trip: Tulsa.

—

MY SOPHOMORE YEAR IN HIGH SCHOOL WE GOT A CALL THAT Booker had had a heart attack while traveling back to Sacramento from Lake Tahoe with my grandma and the now three cousins they took care of. He had stopped to take the snow chains off the Previa. When he got back in the driver's seat his breathing began to pick up pace, and he began wheezing. He grabbed at his chest and passed out in the minivan on the side of the road. My cousins, who were all under nine years old, didn't understand what was happening, but my grandma knew he was having a heart attack. It was poetic in a lot of ways. The van that brought him so much happiness zigzagging the love of his life and his grandchildren all across the country to see and experience the things and places he loved, was the same place Booker Taliaferro Ellis, aka Elgin, aka All Bark and No Bite, aka Grandpa had taken his last breath, during his last road trip.

"You can 'accidentally' staple yourself?"

MY ENTIRE THIRD-GRADE SCHOOL YEAR WAS THE ONLY YEAR in my academic career that I never wanted to be late to class. Mikey and I usually got to the bus stop early, and on the bus I proudly sat right in the front. As soon as the bus screeched to a stop at the entrance of the school, I was first off. I rushed up the stairs and through the double doors into the narrow, yellow-stained, hanging-ceiling-tile hallways of Baty Elementary. I would run as fast as my size-8 feet could carry me, jerking to quick stops when passing any open classroom doors to not get in trouble for running, and once I made it to my classroom, I'd quickly plop into my perfectly positioned front-row desk before any other kids could enter the room. Without fail, just as soon as I took my seat, I'd look up as Ms. Calloway came floating on clouds through the doors.

Ms. Calloway was my third-grade homeroom teacher. So every day—thank God—started with her. She was tall, mocha-skinned, with curly hair and a smile that could have made Saddam and Bush chill out on the Gulf War. I didn't get to class early because I wanted to learn third-grade math or how to make a bean sprout in a plastic bag. I got to class early every day because I had one mission: I was going to make Ms. Calloway my girlfriend.

Once I dropped into my seat, that was the end of my "perfect model student" act. In Ms. Calloway's class, whenever a kid acted up, to keep an eye on them, she would call them to her desk and make them sit next to her the whole period. Most of my classmates saw it as punishment, but to me it was a reward. When I was in that seat, Ms. Calloway would lean in—to tell me to behave—and her endearing and inviting eye contact and her incredible smell would make me Do the Right Thing.

She talked softer when you sat next to her, and it felt like all of my wild-ass, booger-throwing, pissing-on-themselves classmates disappeared as the light from the window wrapped its warm golden rays around her, blanketing Ms. Calloway in an angelic glow. It was euphoric, and exactly what I needed to get me through the school day.

"Ms. Calloway is better than some of the other teachers in the school, sure, but she's old, man! What is she, like twenty-six?" Mikey thought I was tripping. She was twenty-five but I didn't argue. Mikey was a hater who was mad he didn't get any of her attention. But he was still my dude, so he followed up with "You look like a sad lost puppy on a street corner begging for someone to love him, so I guess I'll help you out." Which meant Mikey was about to do something, or convince me to do something, to get me into the seat next to her desk for the rest of the class.

Of the twenty-four kids in class, a little over half were boys—rambunctious, loud, destructive, snot-nosed boys I constantly had to compete with for Ms. Calloway's attention. One of those boys was Lu Tan. Lu could never sit still. He'd always climb onto his desk or crawl behind the coats and backpacks against the back wall. At least three days a week Lu would find himself sitting next to Ms. Calloway, and after a few weeks of Lu taking my rightful throne next to my queen, I realized I had a problem. Lu wasn't just acting out because he wasn't getting enough ass-whoopings at home—kidding!— he was acting out because, like me, he wanted to sit next to Ms. Calloway.

"Lu-Lu got a little thang-thang for your girl," Mikey sang, and he was right. Here I was, thinking Lu was a troglodyte parading as a third-grader, but really Lu was trying to get next to my girl! I realized I would have to do whatever it took to beat Lu to the chair of love, which meant that day after day I'd have to do something bigger and worse than Lu. By any means necessary.

THE NEXT MORNING, AS THE SEA OF MUCUS-SECRETING NOSES AND dirty faces piled into class, I whispered to Mikey, "I need something. But something that won't make her call my parents." I sat in my front-row seat and looked over my shoulder in Lu's direction. He wasn't in his seat yet.

"What about saying you left your books at home?" Mikey said, dropping onto the floor next to me.

"Nah, that won't work. She'll just make me sit next to someone else." Mikey nodded. Any minute, Lu was going to storm in and try to steal my shine.

"You could pee on yourself," Mikey quickly blurted. It was an interesting thought. If I peed on myself, all of the kids in class would make fun of me and maybe she'd move me next to her to make me feel better. But she'd also see me pee on myself and that wouldn't be a good look.

"She won't want me sitting next to her all day smelling like pee," I said.

"You right, you right," Mikey agreed. He eyed the stapler at the front of the room. "You could 'accidentally' staple yourself?" he said, adding air quotes around "accidentally." Before I could respond, Lu walked into class with his slick black hair gleaming, like he'd emptied an entire tube of LA Looks holding gel on it. His chest puffed out and a smirk on his face. I could feel the pressure build up and sit on the back of my neck like the Texas heat in July; I had to do something.

I jumped out of my seat. "Where you going?" Mikey asked, but I was already standing in front of Ms. Calloway's desk. She looked at me with her big, round brown eyes. "How can I help you tod—" Before she could finish, I slid the webbing between my left thumb and pointer finger under the stapler on her desk and, like I was playing Whac-A-Mole at Chuck E. Cheese, I slapped the stapler with my right hand.

There was a collective inhale in the room as I screamed.

"Are you okay?" Ms. Calloway asked, as her eyes widened like two pools of tenderness that I desperately wanted to jump into and swim laps of delightment in.

I was not okay. I had just pounded a staple into my hand. Ms. Calloway reached out and grabbed my hand to inspect it. "You just go down and see the nurse," she said.

Going to the nurse was never the point; it was not an option. Lu would get my seat. I turned to Mikey. He tipped his head toward Ms. Calloway.

What? I mouthed.

"Tell her you want her to do it. Tell her the nurse doesn't like you," Mikey whispered.

"Please . . . don't make me—me—me go to her. She—she—she doesn't like me. Can you just pull—it—out?" I said between gulps of pain. Ms. Calloway should have insisted on sending me to the nurse, but she didn't.

"Sit down and take your notebooks out," she told the class. "I want you to write four sentences about what you did when you got home from school yesterday." Everyone started working on their paragraphs. Ms. Calloway turned back toward me, took a breath, and pulled the staple out of my hand with some tweezers she kept in her bag. Her hands held mine and her eyes were warm like a hug. It hurt like hell but like Mikey always said, "Love hurts."

THE NEXT DAY, ON OUR WAY TO THE BUS STOP, I TOLD MIKEY, "I want a way to say thank you to Ms. Calloway." We kicked ideas back and forth.

"What about a letter?" he asked.

"Then she'll just correct my writing."

Mikey nodded. "You could have her listen to a song on your Walkman."

Not a bad idea, but I had lost the Walkman that Grandpa Booker bought me, so my parents wouldn't let me take the newest one out of the house without permission. And telling my parents I wanted to play the chorus, "If it isn't love, why do I feel this way?" for my homeroom teacher would get me a "Boy, have you lost your ever-loving mind?" followed by deep belly laughter as a response from my mom.

As we waited for the bus, Mikey and I both stared blankly out into the air, waiting for inspiration. Across from the bus stop, one of the houses that faced us had a small rose garden under the living room window. After a beat our eyes landed on the rose garden at the same time. We looked at each other. "Yes!"

Mikey started gassing me to make a run for it. The bus had just turned the corner toward us. I sprinted across the street, trampled through the grass, and searched for the perfect rose—the petals not too open, not too closed, with a deep, dark red color. Fighting my way around the thorns, I plucked a long-stemmed rose. It was beautiful. A little lighter, I ran back across the street and Mikey gave me a fist bump, "Booyah."

I went straight to Ms. Calloway's classroom. My eyes shining like a Lite Brite. I found her unpacking her bag. "Ms. Calloway?" She turned in my direction. I was nervous but Mikey was in my ear whispering what I should do and say: "Relax your shoulders, inhale, and start by thanking her."

"This is for pulling the staple from my hand yesterday and for always being so nice to me."

"Aww, thank you," she said, smiling while she smelled the rose. With Mikey's encouragement, I knew this was the moment.

"Ms. Calloway? I was wondering if you could be my girl-friend already since we love each other?" A shooter's going to shoot. Bless Ms. Calloway's tired and weary public elementary school teaching heart. She looked at me and "Pretty brown eyes," the chorus from "Breakin' My Heart" by Mint Condition, softly played as she walked me over to my desk and sat me down.

"No. No, I will not be your girlfriend. I'm your teacher and I'm too old for you. When you're older you'll find a nice girl your age, and you'll love each other. Until then, I'll be your teacher and you'll be my student." She smiled at me and I tried to smile back as Mint Condition kicked back in: "Quit breakin' my heart . . ."

The rest of the day, Mikey told me joke after joke in an effort to make me stop moping. Eventually his tactics worked, and after the first smile broke across my face, I knew I'd be okay.

It was my first heartbreak, and there were many more, but I put myself out there and learned that allowing that first smile after heartache is the first step toward healing.

Plus, Mikey did come through a few times, and with his help, I did eventually end up with a girlfriend.

—

MY FIFTH-GRADE GIRLFRIEND, NATASHA, AND I SAT NEXT TO each other on the bus to school every morning. Each day, before we'd get on the bus, Mikey and I would run through turn-by-turn scenarios of the thirty-minute route to school. My soul for real opened as "Do you ever dream of candy-coated raindrops?" bounced between my ears.

"Should I try to kiss her when we turn onto Elroy Road?" I'd ask. Mikey's face would frown so hard he'd get pug-like wrinkles between his nose and his forehead.

"Kissing and holding hands is what old people do! It's gross. Ugh." He had issues with PDA.

When Natasha got on the bus, a few stops after me, we spent most of our ride talking about school, our favorite shows (mine, *Inspector Gadget;* hers, *Where in the World Is Carmen Sandiego?*) and what we were going to do at recess (me, play basketball; her, jump rope). It was blissful.

My yellow bus ride-or-die love with Natasha was short-lived. One day, about four months into our green-vinyl-seated love affair, Natasha's parents split up. That morning, Mikey and I had picked the third row back. We had deduced that it was the best seat on the bus, not too close to the bus driver and not too far back that one of her girls could distract Natasha before she got to us.

Natasha climbed on the bus that morning with shoulders rounded. She moved a little slower than usual. Head down, she gingerly slid into the seat next to me. My eyes quickly rolled to Mikey. He shrugged.

"What's wrong?" I asked.

"I can't go to this school anymore."

"What? Why?"

Natasha, head still hanging, mumbled, "My mom is moving to my grandma's house and I have to go with her." Natasha's eyes watered. The world around me slammed to a stop. My ears rang and I struggled to find words. I wasn't emotionally equipped to handle a sudden fifth-grade breakup, let alone a family being split up.

Mikey moved to the seat behind me, leaned over, and whispered in my ear. I took a breath and said I was sorry. The world began to fall back into its normal rhythm. I looked over to Natasha and repeated Mikey's next words with a half smile.

"We'll always have the bus." I don't know if it had a lasting impact or not, but in that moment her body eased and she smiled, her first smile of the day.

BY EIGHTH GRADE, I HAD STARTED DATING MY NEXT GIRLFRIEND, who coincidentally looked like Scary Spice (Mel B). My dad would always joke that she was named after a city in Southern California. She wasn't. She was named after her dad. For a month, my girlfriend (let's call her "West Covina") and I talked about having our first kiss, which we decided would take place after school, before we got on our separate buses home.

This wasn't going to be just my first kiss with West Covina, it was my first kiss ever! The last time I'd seen two people have their first kiss was when Joe Willie of my previous middle school "kissed" Charmaine on the rotted outdoor lunch tables—it looked like he was trying to eat her face. There was no way in hell Joe Willie could've been doing it right, but his sloppy crazed example was the only real-life one I had. Needless to say, I was TERR-I-FIED!

What if I was a bad kisser? I'd never done it before. It was very possible! What if the whole school ended up watching? Have you met middle school kids? These kids were going to ROAST me! You could put a middle school kid up against the most dangerous and threatening animal on the planet and the middle schooler would come out flossing their teeth from the carnage they caused. Would a teacher see? If so, would they send me to a counselor to talk about my feelings after? Also: I was for sure going to have bad breath! I wouldn't have brushed my teeth since seven in the morning, and the food that came out of my school's cafeteria—indistinguishable sauces and unidentifiable mounds of protein—couldn't produce a good aftertaste. I was panicking.

By this time Mikey was kind of like the Hormone Monster in *Big Mouth*. So he gave me a few pointers:

- "The more tongue the better."
- "Chew on a mint before you kiss, not for fresh breath, but because it gives a tingle to the girl's tongue."
- "Make sure you have a lot of spit in your mouth so the kiss is extra wet."
- "Lick your lips before you go into the kiss. It tells the girls you're ready."

Unfortunately, or fortunately, all of my stress and worrying ended up being for nothing. West Covina and I never actually kissed. For a week or so we'd miss each other at the end of school every day where the buses lined up. One of us always had to load in because the bus driver would be yelling, "Last chance! I'm leaving!" Most days I'd watch as she pancaked her face against the window and waved to me, the bus pulling away. My eyes pleading, *Tell me what you want, what you really, really want*. Eventually we broke up because middle school relationships are shorter than middle schoolers' attention spans. I held on to Mikey's advice through high school, my dating life post-Mikey fully shaded by all the things he taught me while he was still around. Even though he didn't have a physical manifestation or a voice in my head, I was making decisions that were influenced by my days with him.

Like, if she splits dinner with you on the first date, she's "The One." Or, if you pop a girl's bike tire and then offer her a ride home on your handlebars, she'll tell all her friends how you saved her and you're "The One."

My junior year in high school, while blending fruit and boredom at my ~~soul~~ ice-crushing job at Smoothie King, LaNisha walked through the doors. LaNisha was spicy. She had a tiny frame but that didn't stop her from popping off on anyone who she felt stepped out of line. She had an uncanny talent for being able to talk shit with the guys, and the esteem she held for herself made everyone around her think twice about disrespecting her. With LaNisha, you had to come correct. Her ability to tolerate bullshit was lower than somebody's drunk aunt doing the limbo at a cookout. She had a part-time job and drove a massive SUV that she could barely see over the steering wheel of. As far as a potential girlfriend, she checked a lot of boxes—boxes Mikey and every hip-hop video from the '90s (As the great American poet Juvenile would say "Girl you look good . . ." You know the rest.) planted in my head.

Although, there was one box she didn't check that I didn't think to ask about.

Without looking at the menu, she ordered two smoothies: a Peanut Power Plus Strawberry and The Activator, with a smile hanging on the side of her face. *Who is this girl? How could she know the menu well enough to not even look at it?*

"So, you been here before?" I asked, thinking *And if so, how did I miss you?* Her eyebrows raised slightly.

"Been in before," she said, with little eye contact and no pleasantries.

"Yeah, me too." I nodded. She looked in my direction and smiled. The voice in my head whispered, *Good one, Jellis.*

I used the time it took me to scoop the ingredients into

the blender to think about how I could get this girl's number. My emotionally undeveloped teenage Neanderthal brain was 100 percent dedicated to getting LaNisha's number. I didn't stop to wonder if she wanted to engage with me enough to even consider giving it to me, nor did I think about how she probably didn't want to be bothered or put on the spot and would rather just get her two smoothies and move on with her day.

"You always drink two smoothies?"

LaNisha's eyes lasered in on my name tag, then moved to lock with mine.

"'Jay,' is that your name?"

"Yeah." I nodded. She moved toward the register on the other end of the store, her back to me the whole time.

"Only way to know is to see me around more." She smirked. I dropped the ice scoop into the freezer. *Don't fuck this up. She just told you to ask her out!*

I placed the blenders on their stations. "I should see you more, huh?" I asked over the loud whirring noise. LaNisha shrugged her shoulders as if to say, *Guess so.* "Well you gotta give me your number then." The blenders stopped. I grabbed two large Styrofoam cups and filled them up. By the time I walked to the register, she had already written her number down on a napkin. She slid it my way and said, "Your turn."

FROM THEN ON, LaNisha AND I HUNG OUT THREE, MAYBE FOUR days a week. When we were together it was like Method Man and Mary J. Blige were there singing, "You're all I need to get by." It was always easy. We'd either meet up at her house, when her parents weren't home, or she'd meet me at the end of my shift slinging sugar smoothies. We'd grab food, talk shit to each other, sit in the back of a movie theater, or ride around town searching for a place to park and chill.

We never hung out with friends or double-dated. We never even bumped into friends on the rare occasions we were out. But I never really noticed, and we were happy with just the two of us kicking it.

During that same time, I didn't hang out with some of my boys much—young love trumped friends—including Malachi. Malachi was one of my best friends. We met two weeks after I moved to Tulsa through his cousin Wayne, who lived in the same apartment complex as me. Whenever Malachi would come over to Wayne's house, we'd all go play in the dumpsters together. Malachi was ridiculously charming; everyone liked him. He could talk soccer with white kids and the latest Rocawear with Black kids.

And although his crossover was a little slow, he had a decent jumper, which made him the Fresh Prince of our school.

We'd usually meet up after the bell rang and run the Tulsa streets, but, like me, he was spending all his time with his new girl after school. We still saw each other in school every day, so even though we weren't running to the mall or Cicis Pizza as much, neither of us thought anything of it.

One night, LaNisha and I decided to go see *House on a Haunted Hill* at the dollar movie theater. We got there a little late because I had to do inventory that night at Smoothie King. By the time I bought candy, drinks, and popcorn, like Mikey taught me, we were the last ones in the theater. We settled in our seats as the opening scene was just starting. About twenty minutes into the haunting, the movie took a turn. Eddie, played by Taye Diggs, showed up to save Sara (Ali

Larter) from a ghost impersonating Eddie, who was trying to drown her in a tank of blood. LaNisha lifted the armrest and leaned closer to me. For the next sixty minutes or so, LaNisha went back and forth between covering her eyes, turning into my shoulder, or wrapping my arm tighter around her. I was in heaven.

When the movie ended, we moved out the double doors toward the lobby and someone called out, "Aye! Jay-E!" Jay-E was a nickname most of my boys called me because it was a play on Jay-Z, who was, and still is, my favorite rapper *and* the greatest rapper of all time. I turned to see Jalen, my boy from another school who was an amazing football player, and his girlfriend, Yvonne, coming out of the same theater as us. As they approached us, with every step Jalen's eyes grew bigger and bigger. His facial expression changed from a familiar smile to a look of concern and confusion.

"Y'all just saw the movie?" he said.

"Yeah." I nodded.

"That's what's up. Who this?" He pointed to LaNisha. "This who been keeping you locked up?" LaNisha and I chuckled, then she introduced herself. At the same time, a pain in my bladder made me remember that I'd needed to pee during the movie but because of LaNisha's death grip, I never got up to go.

"I'ma run pee real quick," I told the group. Jalen quickly announced that he'd come too. As soon as we landed one urinal apart, an unspoken men's room rule of the time, Jalen said, "Aye, you know ya boy not try'na be in your business or nothin' like that, but you know Malachi got a girlfriend named LaNisha too," he said.

"Oh, word?" I asked. "That's random." Malachi had always referred to his girlfriend as "my girl," never naming her, and my teenage brain was too wrapped up in my own love life to even think to ask.

Jalen turned and looked at me. I could feel his eyes demanding contact. I slightly glanced toward him. "You ever met Malachi's girl? Y'all hang out together?"

"Nah, we both been busy," I said, but Jalen's tone made me pause. Malachi and I had never hung out with our girls at the same time. I hadn't hung out with LaNisha's friends and none of my boys had met her until now. And when LaNisha couldn't hang out, neither could Malachi. Jalen looked at me and nodded as I started to connect the puzzle pieces of his questions.

Jalen told me that LaNisha went to his school. He didn't know her but he'd seen her around. His junior class was twelve hundred kids. So it was easy to recognize someone but not know them. Jalen had only met her once at a house party, but he thought he had seen her and Malachi out together a few times too. He was sure it was her.

As he spoke, I could feel myself start to sweat, my world beginning to fuzz. I was pissed. I was in shock. I was confused. I was dumbfounded. My stomach started to hurt. A piercing whale-sound rang through my ears. My seventeen-year-old swagged-out psyche was smashed into a million tiny pieces in that AMC restroom. I was shocked that I hadn't seen any of the signs and had spent so much time with someone who was lying to me. Heartbreak sucks at any age, but when you find out you and one of your friends are dating the same girl, your world turns upside down.

My gut usually protected me from slipping. If I missed the red flag for some reason, my subconscious would pop in: *I don't know, man. Something don't seem right.* Did I ignore it? If Mikey was there, would he have let me ignore it?

"What you gon' do? You want me to handle it?" Jalen asked, snapping me back to the room.

"Nah, I got it," I said, looking up at him. I knew the minute I put Jalen's puzzle together, what I needed to do.

As much as I loved my guy for being willing to handle it for me, I needed to handle this myself. I needed to set my own boundaries and confront her myself.

As soon as Jalen and I stepped back out to the lobby, I immediately saw the shift in LaNisha's body language. The story her eyes and shoulders were now telling was dramatically different from earlier in the theater. Jalen grabbed Yvonne's hand and said, "Let's get outta here," then turned to me. "Hit me if you need anything." He didn't say anything to LaNisha, who mumbled "Bye" under her breath.

I was so pissed and confused, I couldn't make eye contact with her and I wasn't sure what to say or where to start. Luckily, I didn't have to.

"He told you about Malachi?" LaNisha asked.

"Yep." I nodded.

"Can I explain?" she asked. I looked at her, and walked toward the front doors. She trailed behind. After we made our way to the parking lot, she waited until there was no one in sight to begin.

I learned the power of silence that night, because the less I said, the more she wanted to say. She wanted, and perhaps needed, to fill the space. The discomfort of being caught and making amends is often painful and awkward, and owning up to your own behavior, especially at first, can come off as defensive, singular, not for the other person's benefit. She apologized; she cried; she claimed she was confused and didn't know Malachi and I were friends.

There's no way I would have ever turned on my boy; that was a lesson I learned when Mikey was still around. After a while—when her tears and words ran out—there was nothing left to say except "Lose my number." She drove off and I walked home.

THE NEXT MORNING, I HIT MALACHI AND TOLD HIM I'D PICK HIM up on the way to school. When I hopped in my gold 1985 Jeep Grand Cherokee and turned on the radio, a piano riff moved through the 12-inch JBL subwoofers I had in the back, and a silky falsetto voice came in, "Ohhhhh . . . Yeahh yeah . . . Don't wanna beeeeee a player . . ." "Still Not a Player" by Big Pun featuring Joe filled the Jeep—a small sign, perhaps from Mikey, wherever he was. I told Malachi the whole story. I found out that Malachi didn't know either; she had been playing the both of us. LaNisha was the epitome of "I'm not a playa, I just crush a lot." And although I got over it later, at that moment she had crushed me. I learned a lot more about myself during that experience. It was trial and error for the next few years, but with each relationship I learned to keep trying, to keep showing up, for myself, my friends, and whoever I was entangled with. I learned the questions to ask and the signs to look for. It was like fine-tuning the type of people I wanted in my life, and the folks who didn't deserve me.

WHO YOU TALKIN' TO?

AUSTIN, TX

"Yo' ass would be in theater. Ol' *Men in Tights* ass. Ahhhh."

"**R**IC FLAIR IS THE GREATEST WRESTLER TO EVER GRACE THE squared circle. Period!" Mikey declared. With an eye roll and a sigh, I slammed my locker door and walked away from his hot take.

"Are you crazy?! The Rock gives out the People's Elbow like a priest gives Walmart-brand grape juice at Communion. Everybody can get some!" I responded without breaking stride or looking over at him. Mikey, who was clearly still living in 1987, the height of Ric Flair's power and ability, was not having it, though.

"Dude, I'm starting to think you don't know wrestling," he pleaded as he followed me into the restroom—a stop I always made before my third period, seventh-grade math class with Mrs. Mahan, to both relieve myself of all the government-provided public school orange juice I drank for breakfast and to make sure my hair looked good and my breath didn't stink, because I sat next to my crush, Terri Okoto.

I slammed the stall door in the restroom shut, but my blatant signal for privacy didn't matter to Mikey. He banged on the door and yelled, "Wooooo," Ric Flair's signature call. Exasperated with his antics and trying to concentrate, I yelled through the stall door, "Ric Flair, at best, may win a superlative for Best Dressed but there is no way he could beat The Rock one-on-one. Do you smell what I'm cooking?"

I FELL IN LOVE WITH WRESTLING BECAUSE TO ME, WRESTLERS WERE all acting out their imaginary friends' personas in "characters" they created. I figured Dwayne Johnson's imaginary friend growing up was probably "The Rock," a no-nonsense, eyebrow-raising, bronze-skinned, Speedo-wearing hella-Hawaiian-tattoo-having badass who put his elbow in people's mouths to shut them up. Ric Flair's imaginary friend was most likely "Nature Boy," a kid wearing elaborate jewel-draped robes who screamed every time he was allowed to go outside. As grown men they dressed up in ornate costumes, created personality traits and signature wrestling moves, and became internationally known megastar wrestlers. But what if it really all started with their imaginary friends?

"I think if you looked at his body of work . . . you'd . . . think . . ." Mikey slowed to a stop. I should have known by his trailing off and long silence that something was up, but I was so caught up in defending the national treasure that is Dwayne "The Rock" Johnson, I missed all the warning signs. As soon as I zipped, flushed, and bopped out of the stall, I found Mikey covering his mouth and standing behind Ronny, our school's bully.

Ronny was fifteen going on thirty-five, with the muscular-

ity of a football player in his sophomore year of high school—
because he was supposed to be one. He had been held back
twice, once in fifth grade and now doing his second time
around the sun as a fifteen-year-old eighth-grader. If I had to
describe him as a television character, it would be Stringer
Bell.

Before this point, I had never been bullied. Bullies in my
previous schools focused their misplaced angsty energy else-
where, but with Ronny you never knew who he was going to
go after; everyone was fair game.

I froze as soon as I stepped out of the stall—no lie, I
thought about going back in, but I didn't think I was fast
enough to get in or strong enough to hold the door with Ronny's teenage Stringer Bell strength pushing it back open. I
went silent. My body started to heat up and itch, like when
you're sick and your skin feels like a bajillion tiny needles pok-
ing you. If I showed any signs of fear, Ronny would smell it
with his superhuman Stringer Bell senses and pick on me forever. He stood there with a cocky grin. He looked around and
when his faux search ended, he asked:

"Who da fuck you talking to?"

"Me? Uhmm . . . no one." Clearly, I was fast on my toes.

"Stop lying . . . I Just heard your square ass talking 'bout
wrestling."

This wasn't the first time someone caught me talking to
myself. Growing up with an imaginary friend, you often find
yourself in very animated and overly dramatic conversations
and arguments with someone that no one else can see or
hear. For you it's just a normal day, nothing to write home
about. For the world around you, it's a problem that will, unfortunately for you—and by you, I mean me—bring a lot of

judgmental looks, unsolicited advice on how to "fix" ~~it~~ your-self, and demands for an explanation.

"Oh! That . . . I . . . was just—saying this thing I had to re-member for class."

"What class?"

Silence. I could hear my own eyes blinking. Mikey, posi-tioned just over Ronny's shoulder, made all sorts of gestures—most of which I couldn't make out, but it looked like he was performing a one-man play.

"Theater class. It's . . . a, uh, monologue thing for my the-ater class."

"Yo' ass would be in theater. Ol' *Men in Tights* ass. Ahhhh." He bawled with laughter.

The wrestling gods protected me that day. Ronny was so entertained—imagining me wearing tights (no comment), performing my fake monologue—that he just shook his head and left the bathroom. *Why was he in here in the first place?* I released my balled fist and exhaled.

I turned to Mikey and said, "You know I would have given Ronny the People's Elbow," to which Mikey rolled his eyes, put his arm around me, and continued his never-ending argu-ment about the Nature Boy. Before we left the bathroom, we settled on Best Wrestler: The Rock; Best Dressed: Ric Flair.

Mikey, of course, never cared that people were watching and judging. Whenever he had the chance to grandstand, he wanted to go bigger and louder to prove a point. He liked an audience. He lived for it. This pretty much left me looking like I had a mental illness, which is no laughing matter, but when you're a young kid in a new school with no alliances, you can easily become the laughingstock of that school . . . or multiple schools, in my case. It took a while, but Mikey taught me how not to give a f$*k. In all his performativity was a lesson on being comfortable in my own skin. The ultimate "Do you!"

—

FOR A WHILE MY MOM WORKED TWO JOBS, ONE AT THE YMCA and the other at Brooks Fashions (look them up! '80s and early '90s fashion at its peak!). From time to time she would have to take me with her to work. Going to work with my dad was cool but I wasn't allowed to do much—by "much," I mean I couldn't roam freely around a bunch of multimillion-dollar F-16 jets whose engines could char my body in seconds. And even though I was in wonderment the entire time I hung out with my dad at work, there was something special about being left to my own devices at the mall where my mom worked.

My mom wasn't naive. She wasn't just letting me roam around the mall, but at the same time she was a busy sales associate on the floor trying to get commissions and could only keep track of so much. So I'd take advantage while she was preoccupied.

The first handful of times I went into exile in the stockroom of Brooks Fashions weren't that bad. All the ladies who worked with my mom thought it was sweet that she brought me to work. It was inevitable that one of them would walk in while Mikey and I were playing hide-and-seek and ask what I was doing. I'd respond by telling them I was "playing with Mikey." You could literally see their cortisol levels spike as panic set in that there was someone else in the stockroom.

After a cautious beat or two of looking around and asking me where he was, they'd realize I was talking about an imaginary friend. A sigh would give way to a chuckle of relief, and then they'd tell my mom it was cute that I still played with an imaginary friend.

On one particularly long stint of going with my mom to work, I grew accustomed to hanging in the back and trying to peek through the curtain to see what was happening with the people on the floor. I needed those slivers of human life through the curtain, because Mikey and I were spending our days in the back with a bunch of terrifying stiff mannequins. Mikey became friends with the mannequins, who, after some time of him getting to know them, told him how Ms. Cathy—my mom's coworker, who always wore blue eye shadow and big Texas hair—was a great cook who loved to share the lunch she packed every day. She apparently just loved when people loved her food. *Well*, Mikey thought, *there's only one way for her to love that we love her cooking.*

Mikey and I tiptoed through the stockroom into the office and found the dorm-sized refrigerator tucked away under a shelf with plastic utensils, prepackaged Heinz ketchup, and sweet-and-sour packs from the mall's food court. I was like Indiana Jones when I opened the fridge. Shining bright in our faces was the glowing gold statue from *Raiders of the Lost Ark*. Ms. Cathy's food was front and center, surrounded by old weight-loss shakes, fast food, and stuff that looked like it had been in there before Brooks was into fashion. It was also clear that Ms. Cathy loved a Tupperware party, because she had matching containers, and back in the day, you only had matching sets after going to or hosting a party. I love "multi-level marketing" companies, by the way.

On Ms. Cathy's menu for the day were chicken enchiladas. Mikey and I each took a whiff after I cracked open the coordinated Tupperware. Even cold they smelled good. Mikey whisper-yelled while he peeked out the curtain to make sure no one was coming, "Hurry up and microwave it before somebody comes in!" That should have been the very red flag I needed to see that what we were doing wasn't okay, but I was blinded by hunger. My right hand yanked the tiny dorm-sized microwave open and my left hand shoved the enchiladas in. I worked that microwave so fast, I could have set a Guinness World Record. After watching the enchiladas spin around the radiation box for the longest fifty-nine seconds ever recorded, I yanked the door open just before the timer sounded off and gave Mikey and me away. We grabbed a Publix-brand paper plate and two forks, divided up the mouthwatering cheesy, hot enchiladas, and went to town.

Ms. Cathy *could* cook. Mannequins tell no lies. She put her foot all the way in those enchiladas, let me tell you. As we finished destroying Ms. Cathy's enchiladas, another of my mom's coworkers, Ms. Deborah, came in and spotted us. She smiled, not thinking anything of it, and asked, "Mmmh, looks good, was it?" and with a mouth full of happiness and a greasy face I replied, "Yes ma'am!"

Ms. Deborah went out and told my mom I was eating lunch, and within seconds my mom was in the office giving me the business for eating someone else's food.

"Why would you do that? Huh? You hear me talk—"

Ms. Cathy walked in for a stock check. "Hey, Paula, do you know where the—" but stopped as soon as she saw my tongue making out with her Tupperware, licking it clean.

I explained to my mom and Ms. Cathy that one of the

mannequins told Mikey that Ms. Cathy was a good cook who wouldn't mind if we had some. I pointed in Mikey's direction but they just saw an extra plate of food. My mom's eyes rolled so hard, they're probably still rolling now all these years later. Ms. Cathy, sensing the tension, nodded toward the plate.

"There's a little left over. Do you think Mikey would mind if I finished his?" Ms. Cathy asked. She wasn't even mad. I leaned over and asked Mikey—had to double-check my boy wasn't going to starve later, because there was no way in hell my mom was buying us lunch from Whataburger in the food court that day.

"Mikey said he would like for you to have his enchilada."

Ms. Cathy smiled at me and placed an unfolded napkin over the plate.

When I got home I was confined to my room and told to write *I WILL NOT EAT OTHER PEOPLE'S LUNCH* five hundred times as punishment. All the while, I kept thinking how Ms. Cathy didn't raise her voice or look at me crazy; in fact, she did the opposite—she smiled and gave me care. Maybe she really did love when people loved her cooking. Or maybe she just understood play and imagination. From then on, each time my mom took me to work, her coworkers would say hi to Mikey and ask him to not eat their lunches.

—

As I got a little older my parents' patience with Mikey began to wear thin. Mainly because I was always causing trouble or making a mess. My dad repeatedly let me know that I looked like a "fool" when I was out in public fighting with "myself."

With a few exceptions and for as long as I can remember, my dad has worked in, on, or around fighter jets and airplanes. Sometimes his office, also known as an airplane hangar, would become Mikey's and my playground—the fighter jets, tools, and other miscellaneous government-owned items would often serve as set decoration and props.

I went to work with my dad once during parent-teacher conference day. That meant one thing and one thing only: Mikey and I were going to have the chance to fly! A rush of wind smacked us in the face as the giant doors of an airplane hangar opened. The smell of jet fuel hit my nose, going straight to my brain, igniting all the ideas Mikey and I had for taking flight that day.

My dad walked us into the office just off the open hangar. The office was filled with huge metal furniture that was probably cutting-edge back in the '50s. He sat me down in a rolling *and* spinning chair, and said, "Stay in here, and if you need something come get me." I saluted, and with a smirk on his face, he walked out.

Immediately, Mikey and I grabbed a couple self-peeling pencils, a few sheets of graph paper, two binders that had *F-16* written on them above a picture of a jet, and the sunflower seeds that were tempting us on an adjacent desk. I'm not sure if it was the jet fuel or the purple Kool-Aid I snuck a sip of at breakfast, but hours felt like seconds. I was limitless. Mikey and I were deep in the calculations and modeling we'd need to fly.

I was the Black Neil Armstrong and Mikey the Black Buzz

Aldrin of our time. We scribbled on graph paper and then realized the flaws in our calculations. *Houston, we have a problem.* We balled up our computations and started again. Whenever we got stuck, Mikey would say, "Go for a spin?" He would then jump behind my chair and spin me as fast as he could until my mind was clear—I was dizzy—and I could re-approach the problem, after catching my balance.

Another little life lesson Mikey slyly slid in: Sometimes you have to clear your mind in order to see something with fresh eyes and resolve the issues frustrating you.

An hour later we had eaten through the entire bag of sunflower seeds and discarded the shells all over the coffee-stained, green-and-white-checkered linoleum floor. Our pencils were worn down to stubs, with the shavings covering the desk, and balls of paper littered the room, but then, *BAM!* We finally figured it out. We solved what my dad and all those highly trained engineers, mechanics, and pilots had spent years in school learning, and decades practicing and implementing—we figured out how to fly. And the only thing we needed wasn't years of training, anything the Wright brothers invented, or an understanding of physics, mathematics, the theory of flight, jet fuel, propellers . . . We just needed magic.

After confirming the coast was clear—my dad and his buddies were out smoking cigarettes—we opened the heavy metal office door and creeped into the hangar. We searched in toolboxes, under the jets, in the green crates along the walls, but we couldn't find what we were looking for—until Mikey found a sheet of paper with times and signatures hanging on a door. This was it. The magic we were looking for had to be behind the door.

"You have to sign for everything top secret. That's how they know who goes in and out and who's seen it last," Mikey whispered. Damn, he was smart! I slowly opened the door and there in the back of the small, dark, and damp room was what all of our calculations, drawings, and modeling had sent us on a search to find. I pulled it out and held it to the sky like it was baby Simba in *The Lion King,* and I was presenting it to the gods of flight. This one thing, this magical relic that man had searched far and wide for, this thing that represented freedom and independence, the thing that was going to take me anywhere I wanted to go, was a long, thin, but still substantial push broom.

Mikey and I loaded on and took flight. It was only a few short minutes, but we flew all over Texas—down south over the Alamo and zipping over Arlington through Six Flags—all the way to Florida, over my great-grandparents' house in Tampa. We covered a lot of ground in under ten minutes.

Midflight, my dad and his coworkers came in through the side door of the hangar from their break. They all stood at the end of the room staring in my direction as I hopped around, flying a "magical" push broom that was probably ordered from a government catalog.

What I saw was me and Mikey using our imagination and believing in ourselves, proving to the world that we could fly. What my dad and his coworkers saw was a boy straddling a broom, screaming "The air is so cold up here!" and "Look at Disney World down there!" to his imaginary friend.

"Wendell!" my dad yelled—he only used my government name when he was pissed. He screamed for me to get down off the portable staircase I was standing on.

With each step down, the lush green foliage and salty blue

waters of the Gulf quickly washed away and faded to a run-down, gray metal airplane hangar. The smells of ripe citrus fruits gave way to the pungent, face-scrunching fragrance of jet fuel fumes. I was so consumed by what Mikey and I had created that nothing in that hangar mattered or existed anymore. I had found freedom, flight, and myself fully engulfed in joy.

My dad wasn't angry about my imaginary friend or my very short imaginary flight. He wasn't upset about my dream-like fantasy. He was pissed because I was swinging the "magical" broom all over the hangar, hitting people and knocking things over that he'd have to clean up. Mikey and I were making more work for him and his buddies, after my dad had snuck me in while his boss, Master Sergeant Don't Remember His Name, was gone. I hadn't even noticed Mikey and I had hit anyone, or that we had spilled a giant vat of oil. My pops was angry I was being reckless and oblivious of my surroundings. Not to mention the fact that because of my lack of spatial awareness, I could have seriously hurt myself.

EVEN THOUGH I GOT PUNISHED FOR EATING MS. CATHY'S ENCHI-ladas and making a mess of the hangar, I knew Mikey and I were onto something—and so did my parents. Creativity, like freedom, can scare folks, because both lead to us becoming brighter and bigger versions of ourselves. Although I got all the smoke in the moment, my parents knew Mikey was nurturing my imagination; and, not all the time but usually, they wanted to empower this. People are intimidated by what they can't see or understand. I didn't have to roll out the People's Elbow back in that rancid-smelling school bathroom, because

Ronny didn't know how to respond. He shook his head and left the bathroom after I told him I was acting out a monologue.

My parents may not have fallen for all my schemes, but I ended up with something just as good if not better—a playground for my imagination, which has led to a career "playing out" my imagination. I went from imagining flying jets back in that hangar in Austin, Texas, to literally flying jets in movies. The ingenuity and creativity Mikey brought into my life taught me how to prioritize and wield my imagination, and just how powerful it can be.

—

BECAUSE OTHER FOLKS CAN'T SEE YOUR IMAGINARY FRIEND, AND people tend to be uncomfortable with things they can't see and can't explain, they often form thoughts around the rules and even recommended social graces of the imaginary-friend community to make it make sense for themselves. Like: *Having an imaginary friend means you can see other kids' imaginary friends.*

MY GREAT-AUNT BETTINA BACK IN STOCKTON WAS A FOSTER MOM. She always opened her home and family to someone who needed stability and love. Whenever my parents shipped me off to Sacramento to be with my grandparents for the summer, Nana would occasionally send me and my cousin Destiny down to Stockton to visit my cousins and great-aunt, who'd usually have a different foster child than the previous summer. The cousins—we have a small clan there; about twenty people on my mom's side—were all girls. I was the only boy on that side of the family, and the youngest, for a long time. Torture. When we visited, Mikey and I would do whatever we could to hide from them, because they would either try to punk me or get me to play with them, however *they* wanted to play—no, thank you.

On one particular visit, my cousins were ecstatic for me to meet Damon, that summer's foster kid, because Damon also had an imaginary friend. As soon as I stepped foot into my aunt's house—the air smelled of fried chicken and hot combs on the stove—my cousin Sameera declared that the girls always heard Damon talking to his imaginary friend. And because they knew I had an imaginary friend (no shame in my game when it came to talking about my boy Mikey), Sameera told me the cousins had devised a plan for me to decipher if Harry was real, or if Damon just liked talking to himself.

The next day, the cousins huddled up hushed outside Damon's door. They wrapped me in their arms like a toddler clutching a teddy bear so I couldn't move away. Their plan worked flawlessly. As soon as these mischievous little humans, dressed in their frilly dresses with hair laid, heard Damon talking to Harry, they swung the door open, shoved me into the room, and locked me in. Two of my cousins, twins—Aisha and Patricia—yeah, I'm calling y'all out—were the ones who threw me into my potential demise. I tried to fight it, I did, but there's something in the Stockton water that made them strong. I kicked and screamed but it was no use. The door was slammed in our face. Through the door they yelled for me to "see what Harry looks like and tell us."

Because I had an imaginary friend, they assumed I should

be able to see all the imaginary friends of other people. I yelled back that that isn't how it works, but my efforts were fruitless, they barricaded the door, and now their plan was fully under way. I was locked in a room with Damon . . . and maybe Harry.

As I tiptoed deeper into the room, I could hear all the girls leaning on the door and shushing each other. Damon had his back turned to me, facing the wall. He had been quiet during the commotion of the cousins throwing me into his room, but within seconds he began talking to someone in the closet. The collective four and a half hairs on my arms and legs stood up. I slowly turned to look around the room and saw the biggest green and hairy—nah, I'm lying—I didn't see anything except Damon sitting on the bed, facing the wall and talking to himself.

"Who you talking to?" I said, but he just ignored me and continued his conversation with Harry . . . or the wall. I didn't care that he was having a conversation with his imaginary friend, but I did care that he wouldn't even acknowledge me. We were the only boys in the house and the girls were using us for entertainment—this was our moment to band together! I figured Damon and I could learn to stick together, like I'd done with my aunt and uncle's previous foster kids. I took a heavy step forward, sighed loudly, sucked my teeth—it didn't matter, Damon was flat-out ignoring me and kept all his attention on Harry. The restless girls broke their silence and called out, "What he look like?!" but of course I didn't see Harry, because I didn't imagine Harry; all I saw was Damon's back.

I couldn't see Harry, but I did overhear Damon and his imaginary friend discussing their upcoming plan. Damon didn't speak loudly, so I couldn't move or make noise, because I might miss something. I stood quietly listening to Damon work through his plot to run away. The girls snickered just beyond the door and I debated what to do. I didn't want to be known as a snitch, I didn't want a Stockton doctor giving me stitches, and at that time in Stockton a lot of bodies ended up in ditches—I wasn't trying to be one of them.

If perpetuity could be condensed into a few minutes, that's what it felt like until the cousins finally opened the barricaded door and I was let out of the room. The cousins circled me, leaving no exit, like an Illuminati initiation ceremony, and asked what happened. I hadn't seen Harry, and despite me telling them beforehand I wouldn't be able to, I said it again. They looked at me disapprovingly. Eyes rolled *hard*. Backs of teeth were *kissed*. Hands furiously found their way to hips. I didn't know what else to say to them. I didn't want to tell them about Harry, and I didn't want to be a snitch and tell them Damon was going to run away. So after a few minutes of them annoying the hell out of me with their questions, I blurted out, *"He doesn't have an imaginary friend. He just talks to himself."* The girls clearly thought that talking to himself was *much worse* than having an imaginary friend, because they immediately left to tell Aunt Bettina.

For the rest of the day, Damon and I learned to coexist by spending time together outside—more than either of us planned for that hot and humid weekend.

The weather in Stockton in the dead of summer is no place for kids to be playing outside, for two reasons: 1) The heat and humidity are Deep South levels of "What the fuck?" high, and 2) Stockton is downwind from dozens of cow farms, and in those few hot and sticky moments when there is a breeze, it's impossible to enjoy it because the cow-produced methane gas that pugnaciously invades your nose smells like death. However, my great-aunt didn't want anybody playing in her house.

She would sit in her brown recliner chair, legs tilted up, point her long fluorescent acrylic nails, and tell you you had two options: "Sit on this here floor and be quiet while I watch my stories, or go on outside . . . but you best not leave that yard." The girls always chose inside—they knew better than to get their hair sweaty and a mess and have to endure the hot comb again for church the next day. So with the girls hella scared of getting their ears-tips burnt, Damon and I both knew that being outside was each of our best chance at having a hassle-free Saturday.

We started on opposite sides of the backyard. My great-uncle wouldn't let us go out front because at any time it could pop off—the block was hot, and I'm not only talking about temperature. The backyard was wide and bare, so Mikey and I decided to build an obstacle course. As the morning trickled by, Mikey pushed me to engage with Damon because he thought that, like me, Damon was probably always the only one in the room with an imaginary friend, and therefore I should at least try to talk to him. Ugh, the burdens of having a considerate imaginary friend. So, I yelled across the yard, "It stinks out here, huh?" Damon just barely looked over his shoulder and made a point to turn back to whatever he was doing before I'd interrupted. I turned to Mikey and shrugged. *I tried; clearly he doesn't want to engage.*

In some ways it was comforting. I didn't feel like I had to play with someone I barely knew just because we had imaginary friends in common. It was also a relief knowing that if I blurted something out to Mikey, Damon wouldn't point and laugh in my face. I could just be.

On the other hand, I was salty because this was the second time Damon didn't respond to me, and he should at least acknowledge me, right? I'm a year older, I have an imaginary friend too, I kind of know how to handle the girl cousins, and most importantly I didn't snitch on him! In most hoods, I'd be considered a living legend. At some point, I said to Mikey, "Whatever, he don't wanna be my friend, I don't wanna be his."

I take rejection well.

By midafternoon, Damon and I had slowly moved toward the center of the yard and occupied a little more of each other's space. When Mikey and I finished construction of our mini-swamp for my G.I. Joes' obstacle course, I yelled out, "We need the hose!" Damon, not saying anything, kicked the hose closer to me. Mikey looked at me pointedly and mouthed, *Say thank you.* I looked at Damon then back to Mikey, his hands now pushing me closer to Damon: *Do it.* I turned toward Damon, who sat on the white plastic outdoor table with two small potted plants, a hummingbird feeder, a citronella candle, a Batman action figure with the cape torn off, and a stack of flowers and leaves, and said "Thanks!" Damon mumbled, "Errwellcm."

Sameera poked her head out of the sliding glass door and yelled, "Aunty said y'all need to come in and clean up so we can go." Neither of us wanted to come in, clean up, or go to church for whatever deacon meeting they were dragging us to, but my great-aunt and -uncle both had a mean belt game, so we went inside. As soon as we entered the house full of cousins, I realized being outside with Damon, giving each other space to play and be, was more "fun" and peaceful than any other experience that summer.

Damon, for his own reasons, just wanted to be alone. He enjoyed his own company, and Harry's. I was also comfortable, and enjoyed being by myself . . . as long as Mikey was around. We didn't judge each other.

The next morning, my grandmother whisked me back to Sacramento to cut her grass. All the cousins and Damon—hiding in the back—stood in the front yard and waved bye as we drove away in my nana's gold Nissan—windows down, of course, because "We not wasting no gas on air-conditioning. It ain't that hot."

The next time I was in Stockton, a year later, Damon wasn't there. My great-aunt had opened her home and family to a new kid who needed a new place to find their own peace.

I never saw Damon again, but looking back I rationalized that he probably created his imaginary friend to help him cope with the situation he was in before he got to Aunt Bettina's. I assumed his imaginary friend helped him deal with whatever pain or confusion he felt, as well as being a stable presence as he moved through the foster system in the '90s. We didn't have the same life trajectory, but with moving around so much, Mikey also gave me stability. Maybe somewhere deep in the back of Damon's head he knew that if he made something up—something that might scare others but that he found comfort in, like an invisible friend—he would be left to his own devices, and that he could use his imaginary friend to not only protect himself from the feelings instability triggers, but to give himself a kind of peace and control.

—

IN MY EXPERIENCE, PARENTS AND GUARDIANS OF ONLY CHILDREN are always pushing them to play with other kids—especially when their only child has an imaginary friend. Sometimes it's because they are worried their kid has no interpersonal skills and doesn't know how to be around other kids, which they believe will inevitably lead the child to become a sociopath. Other times it's because a kid and their imaginary friend are destroying everything they touch, and the parents are going crazy and broke trying to clean up the kid's messes. The latter was my parents' reasoning for why, from time to time, they would force me into playing with the kids of some of their friends.

We had been in Oklahoma for about two years and I still hadn't fully adjusted. My acclimation time was as slow as the half Southern/half Midwestern drawl everyone around me spoke with. It was hot and muggy all the time; everything felt slow. We got new music late—except DJ Screw, No Limit, MJG, and Project Pat and Nelly—and the mall stores always felt a season behind. The city was racially split in fourths: Black to the north, upper-middle-class White to the south, lower-income White on the Westside, and a melting pot of Asian, South Asian, African, and Hispanic to the east. Culture shock dripped from every pore of my body. I always felt like I had stepped into an alternate universe in contrast to all of the other places I'd lived before we moved there. Just trying to grab on to something I recognized to ground me. I didn't know how to identify the feeling at the time; instead I walked around for two years with a confused look frozen on my face.

Luckily I had Mikey, and eventually I met a few other kids in school that I vibed with, but they didn't live in the same neighborhood as me, so we really only saw each other at school. On the weekends I was often alone, and my parents (because they couldn't see I was absolutely fine hanging with Mikey) devised plans to set me up with their work friends' kids. Enter Mason.

Somewhere along Mason's path to becoming the next David "Son of Sam" Berkowitz, my parents and his parents became friends, which meant Mikey and I were going to lose perfectly good Saturdays and Sundays doing whatever we wanted.

Mason—thank God, for the sake of all the only children in the world—was not an only child, but he was the youngest child, with two much older siblings. He was short for his age, and had big, round brown eyes that were glazed with a faux kindness sheen. He didn't do well in a barber chair, so his haircuts always looked like a toddler took scissors to his dome. And although he had older siblings, he did not rock their hand-me-downs. His parents made sure he was always in the latest the Gap had to offer.

Being the youngest, Mason was constantly trying to get the attention of his family, but his parents were busy working to occupy his older siblings with things that would keep them out of teenage trouble. So Mason, like a lot of overlooked kids, began to act out. For instance, he and his imaginary friend, Black Knight, tried to light his brother's blanket on fire while the brother was asleep. Not the top of the blanket, but the underside, where his brother's body was.

Mason had an infatuation with fire.

One weekend, my parents decided we'd make the trek out

to Mason's parents' house. I say "trek" because Mason's family lived outside the city, in the suburbs, which at that time meant you were mad successful. And at this point in my life, Mason's parents were definitely two of the most successful Black people I had ever met. They lived in a gated neighborhood. The only people we knew who lived behind gates were behind those gates at the behest of the correctional system. Mikey's face was pressed against the glass as we pulled down perfectly manicured streets. A man-made pond holding the center of the neighborhood together.

"This is the kind of neighborhood Oprah and Michael Jordan live in," I told Mikey, who looked like a dog about to jump out of a window. When we stopped in front of Mason's house, Mikey and I slowly climbed out of the back seat and followed my parents up the long pathway to the front door. Their house was bigger than an elementary school basketball gym, which was the only reference to size I could imagine at the time. As we strolled our way to their door, my mom was giving me a reminder on how I needed to "act right" in other people's houses. She said we needed to play nicely and then added, "Mason has an imaginary friend too. So I'm sure y'all will get along."

Errerehhh! The record of life scratched! Mikey and I looked at each other as what was really happening dawned on us. This was a coup. A setup based solely on the coincidence that Mason and I both had imaginary friends. That's not a strong cornerstone to build the foundation of a friendship. Having an invisible friend is not like sharing a hobby!

As we pushed into the house, Mason's mom stopped just short of the living room in front of a long staircase, and called up, "Mason, they're here! Come down and meet Wendell."

For a beat there was nothing but unnerving silence and then, as if the gates of hell had opened and the devil himself screamed a battle cry, Mason let out a deep, guttural scream. My parents smiled awkwardly. Mason's mom said, "Oh, he's just playing. You can go up and play with him." I turned and looked at my mom, who nodded for me to go up the staircase. It was like a scene from a horror film. I could see it so clearly:

One of the kids from Children of the Corn *has escaped and is living in exile in the attic of a house. His parents love him but are afraid of what the world would do to such an evil, hideous, and destructive beast. So, they lure unsuspecting parents over to barbecue in an attempt to feed the poor, spades-playing, distracted parents' child to their hideous monster of a son.*

By the time I snapped out of my nightmare and turned to look back at my parents, they were gone. It was just me and Mikey looking up at the tallest, longest, scariest staircase we'd ever seen. After a few beats of trying to get each other to go first, we decided to go together, step-by-step. Time slowed. Every time we heard the beast yell, we'd go back down a few steps. Mikey and I vowed that if this was how we were meant to die, we'd do it together. And we wouldn't go out without a fight.

We landed at the top of the stairs with our eyes closed. Neither of us wanted to see the thing that was about to eat us. We slowly opened our eyes and found a small, for his age, kid playing with one of those megaphones that had different voice changers.

Instantly we relaxed, and Mikey made jokes, talking about how he wasn't that scared anyway. Mason asked if I wanted to play. He seemed harmless. We were tripping for nothing. I sat next to him on the floor of his bedroom and grabbed the nearest action figure. Mason quickly snatched it out of my hands and said, "I'm playing with that."

"Okay," I said, and reached for another action figure.

"I'm playing with that!" he yelled, again snatching it out of my hand. Mikey looked at me and tilted his head toward the staircase, signaling for us to get the hell out of there. But I wasn't about to let this little kid punk me. *Hell no, he can't play with all his toys at one time! Nah, son.*

"Well, why'd you ask me over here if I can't play with anything?"

Mason looked up from the two action figures he was crashing into each other.

"'Cause I wanted to trick you into my lair so I can destroy you," he said with a half grin reminiscent of a miniature Ted Bundy. Why this little boy was talking like the archvillain from *Inspector Gadget,* I don't know, but I knew this wasn't going to end well. Mikey and I scooted back into a quick huddle. While we were going back and forth on how we were going to get out of what was sure to be our death, Mason started talking to his imaginary friend, Black Knight, about what was the best instrument available in the room to do the deed. He walked over to his toy chest and after shuffling toys around, he grabbed something, turned quickly around, and started running toward Mikey and me with a Wiffle ball bat in his right hand and the tweezers from the game Operation in his left hand.

"Aye, stop playing. This ain't funny," I said to Mason, as I backed myself into a corner. He slowed down, and stalked up to us like he was a lion prowling in the plains of the Serengeti and we were his prey.

"Mason, if you come over here, I'm gonna punch you in your stupid face."

He flashed his sweet-corn-yellow deranged toothy grin again and kept moving closer. He was less than five feet away and the grin got bigger when I yelled, "Mason! I'm being serious. This the last warning." As soon as I said that he lunged toward me with the bat. Mikey tripped and went tumbling to the floor. I jumped out of the way and Mason began his chase. Mikey and I ran around the room screaming like the first time we saw *Nightmare on Elm Street,* while our parents were downstairs drinking Bartles & Jaymes and playing spades.

I knew the only way out of this situation was to defend myself against "Mason the Menace." I grabbed a pillow off the bed, and one of Mason's action figures from the floor. As soon as I touched the action figure, Mason screamed like a feral cat. I had never heard a human scream like that before; it was otherworldly. As fast as I had picked it up, I threw the toy back on the ground.

Mason dove to the ground to get the action figure and when he did, I jumped on top of him. I smothered his face with the pillow. He tried to fight back but when your head is being held down and you can't see and your breathing becomes restricted, sooner or later you give up. He dropped the bat but tried to stab me with the Operation tweezers. He got my left thigh, a scar I still have. I held the pillow over his face with my right hand, and with my left I tried to pin his arm down to make him drop the tweezers. As I was exerting my impressive and undeniable show of dominance against Mason the Menace, his mom came up, not to save my life from her murderous son, but to see if we wanted any snacks.

"Get off him! What is going on?" she yelled, as soon as she saw me smothering her precious devil. I rolled off Mason, exhausted from defending the Ellis family lineage.

"Mom . . . he said he just wanted to . . . kill me!" Mason said, barely able to breathe, and on cue, he started crying. Real-ass tears. It was the best performance I've ever seen. I'm talking award-worthy, like he was graduating summa cum laude at the Viola Davis and Sterling K. Brown School for Organic Theatrical Crying.

Mason's mom called my mom upstairs. I told the truth of what happened—I had barely been in the room for five minutes before the boy turned on me; I was defending myself. Mikey stood next to me agreeing with everything I said.

"Tell them about the smile, tell them about him trying to trick you into his lair," Mikey said.

My mom was trying not to hear it. I had acted out at someone else's house—the one thing she told me not to do. Mason's mom—who traveled for work a lot, seemed a little blind to the behavioral issues of her chocolate Chucky doll of a son—she couldn't believe the accusations I was making against her maniacal baby boy. My mom made me apologize, and Mason the Menace got the attention he wanted when my parents and I ended up leaving early.

As soon as I got home, my mom put my wrist to work. I had to write sentences: *I WILL NOT SUFFOCATE PEOPLE WITH PILLOWS.*

—

DAMON AND I FOUND OUR BALANCE BUT IT WASN'T JUST BECAUSE we both had imaginary friends; and not only did Mason having an invisible friend fail to impact whether I liked him, or he me, but it also didn't protect me from falling victim to his villainous behavior. A single shared personality trait isn't enough to build a lifelong friendship, but it did help me learn empathy—and that when your gut says *run,* you run.

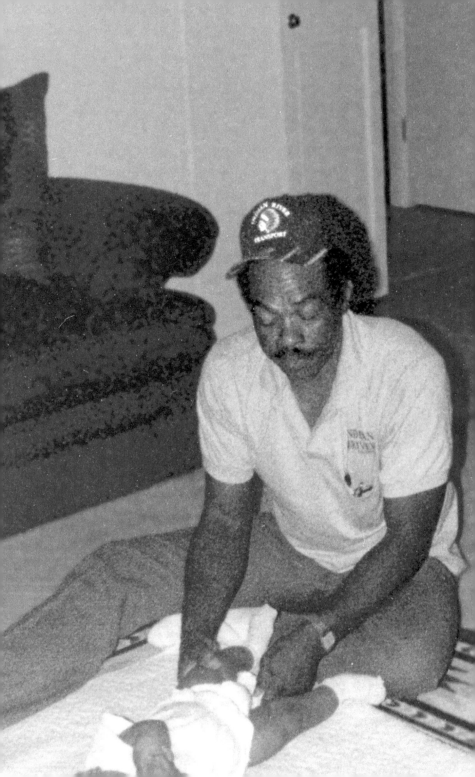

ROLE MODELS

A Truck Stop Somewhere in Central Texas

> "Adopt a lizard baby like the *Enquirer*
> said Hillary Clinton did."

GROWING UP WITH A DAD ENLISTED IN THE AIR FORCE MEANT that we were always at the government's beck and call. Air Force base hopping could feel like torture for a kid, especially an only child. I had to constantly find my grounding, and I had to do it alone. And because of it, I was always in search of role models or mentors.

My parents were cool but they were my parents. And until I got older, that's the only way I could see them. With all my parents had gone through—they were teenage parents who worked hard and sacrificed everything for me—you can imagine it was hard for me to tell them my true dream was to become a movie star. It took me a while to figure out, but with Mikey's help, I did.

When Mikey and I would talk about who we wanted to be when we grew up, all our answers were famous people or cartoon characters. For a time I wanted to be a gunslinger like Wyatt Earp, then an astronaut like Buzz Lightyear, an inventor like George Washington Carver, a singer like Milli Vanilli—"Blame it on the rain, yeah yeah!"—and an NBA superstar like Jordan. Like many kids, all these dreams were just phases of me wanting to be whatever I found interesting at the time, and sometimes whatever other kids at school found interesting. For example, during sixth grade I wanted to be an FBI agent because I overheard a few teenagers at the YMCA say that FBI stood for "Female Body Investigator." *Hello! I just hit puberty! Sign ya boy up, please!* Before I could fully manifest this, I asked my social studies teacher about the FBI and within seconds that dream was crushed. But Mikey always knew that, since I was six years old, my real dream was the one I never said aloud.

To young Jay, a mentor had to be famous or rich or a cartoon character. They had to ooze success in whatever my two-second attention span was interested in at the time. I'm not really sure why I yearned for a mentorship so much. I didn't even know what it was. But I thought everyone was supposed to have one. My mom had mentors at work. My dad had his in the service. I just wanted someone to give me the cheat code so I could follow behind them and get the thing I wanted from a young age. Hollywood.

At the time, I wanted to be in Hollywood for obvious reasons: money, fame, owning a club named after a deadly snake, a pet monkey, an oxygen chamber, never allowing people to look me in the eye . . . you get it. So Mikey, being the great trusted advisor that he was, did everything he could to make sure I was prepared for life in the limelight.

—

AT SEVEN YEARS OLD, LIVING A GALAXY AWAY FROM HOLLYWOOD between Manor, Texas, during the school year and Sac in the summer, Mikey and I didn't really have much to go on about stardom. Neither of us had been to L.A., knew any actors, or had even auditioned for anything. Everything we knew about making it in La-La Land came from the tabloids in the checkout aisles of grocery stores or truck stops; therefore this was our first stop in finding a role model.

I was too young and broke to buy all the gossip mags at whatever Piggly Wiggly or Tom Thumb we were at, but little did I know and luckily for me, my salt-of-the-earth, truck-driving grandpa James had a guilty pleasure for reading conspiracy theory magazines.

The first time Mikey and I saw a Hollywood star we recognized on the cover of one of those magazines was at a truck stop with my grandpa James. It was a feature on a race of space aliens who worshipped Oprah. Grandpa wasn't driving a truck at the time. He had been a truck driver for thirty years, and being on the open road for so long, he preferred going to truck stops on the edges of civilization over going to a gas station in town. I'm not sure if it was the diesel fumes, the way the restrooms always looked like a crime scene and smelled like everyone purposely missed the urinal, or the small talk between truck drivers at the stop, but whatever the draw was, James was always down to drive to Timbuktu and back to find a truck stop. He didn't get down with corner gas stations at all. Too pedestrian for him.

—

FOR A STRETCH OF TIME WHILE WE LIVED IN THE AUSTIN AREA, Grandpa James lived in a North Austin suburb called Round Rock. Grandpa James was slick. A little country. Always wore a mustache and a mesh-backed trucker hat. I've never heard anyone suck their teeth more in one sentence than he would. It was a wonder of the world. On the few random weekends during the school year that Grandpa James was in town and not big-rigging across the country, he'd pick me and Mikey up and we'd spend a day hanging out.

Grandpa James had no idea what to do with a seven-year-old, but he knew me sitting on the floor as he lay back in his La-Z-Boy—big toe hanging out the worn hole in his sock—watching *Shaft* or *Coffy* and smoking a pack of Kool cigarettes, was not the way to go. Because he knew that when my mom asked me what we did and I told her what we did down to every minute of the day, he'd get a phone call about it. Personally, I would have loved to sit around the TV all day, but my mom wasn't having that, so Grandpa James and I would go eat, usually but not always at Kentucky Fried Chicken. He'd order a bucket and, while he ran into a store for more cartons of cigarettes, I'd sneak an extra drumstick and stash the leftover evidence under the car before he came back. But the thing we always did, one of his favorite things to do, was to visit a truck stop.

THE WEEKEND I READ THE FIRST "BOOK" THAT LOCKED IN MY FUTURE dreams of being an actor started with one of those into-the-boonies trips. His preferred stop was north of the city off I-35. The attached convenience store had all of the snacks, drinks, and random junk you could think of. There were also showers, laundry rooms, and quarter massage chairs. I liked to roam up and down the aisles looking for a Slim Jim— thanks to "Macho Man" Randy Savage—and Mountain Dew. Mikey always wanted Funyuns and a Dr Pepper.

Since my grandpa spent so much time on the road, he refused to get a Blockbuster (RIP) membership. So whenever Mikey and I were with Grandpa James and wanted to rent a movie to take notes and study for my future, we'd have to get it at the truck stop.

We stopped in the video section, which carried VHS tapes ranging from PG films like *Cool Runnings* to X-rated titles like *Dr. Butts 3*. I scanned to find a flick we had heard a few older kids talking about a few days earlier, *Coneheads,* but all we could find on the rack was *Boneheads,* and although the actors had cones on their heads, it was where they were sticking the cones that made us realize it wasn't the same movie. We moved on, made a wrong turn or two, and found ourselves walking down a narrow hallway with flickering overhead yellow lights. The walls were bare, and the worn, checkered, black and white linoleum tile was cracked. It was like a scripted horror movie scene; cue deep, creepy, male voice:

Mikey and Jay walk down a dark hallway, the only movement the light twitching. A smoky haze fills the hall—so much so, the far end disappears. A low but commanding thud begins. Mikey and Jay look at each other, the exchanged glance communicating they should turn back. They can't. It's like they are drawn to the sound, hypno-

*tized. Pulled by an invisible force. The closer they move
toward the sound, the louder it gets. The rhythm speeds up.*

There is no clearer signal for DO NOT GO IN ANY FUR-
THER. And yet.

"Maybe we should go back and find your grandpa," Mikey
whispered, but my legs kept moving me forward.

"I have to know what this sound is and where it's coming
from." I kept walking but Mikey didn't move. I became impatient. "Come on, Mikey" (only child syndrome). We creeped
past a doorway, and an odor wafted out that almost bowled us
over. It was like days-old fish and rotted asparagus with a hint
of garlic. It made raw chitlins smell good.

I kept moving, trying to trace the source of the sound,
dragging Mikey along with me. We approached another
door, and as we got closer the sound became louder.

CLUNKKKK'A! CLUNKKKK'A!

A loud laugh mixed with a cough erupted: "Ahahargh."

Mikey grabbed my shoulder. "Maybe it's a zombie pirate
and he's cutting people's heads off?"

I looked at Mikey. "At a truck stop? No! Now open the
door."

Mikey jumped behind me and shook his head. *Hell naw!*

I grabbed the doorknob, said a quick prayer, then slowly
pushed it open. Behind us, the light in the hallway flickered
again. Mikey yelped like a wounded puppy. We peeked through
the crack of the open door, and there in front of us sat the
source of the loud and sinister laughter . . . four truck drivers
sitting at a round plastic table in crumpled plastic chairs, smoking cigarettes while playing poker.

To their left was a row of washers *clunk-clunk-clunking* along as they ran through a wash cycle. It was just a laundry room, and one of the truck drivers clearly had a very moist smoker's cough that he needed to get checked out.

Mikey rolled his eyes like he had learned from the best, my cousins in Stockton. "That was stupid."

He was right. I was positive we were about to stumble on the greatest secret in truck stop history: *how the gas gets in the pumps.* There had to be little gas elves below the ground spinning, wheeling, or pumping a well that extracted gas from the ground and sent it to the gas pumps. We were going to be the first ones to discover them. We were like the little David Attenboroughs of the underground truck stop world. We weren't scared, we were *curious.* But nah, it was four fast-food-eating, chain-smoking card sharks washing their funky clothes.

Disappointed that we'd missed the discovery of a lifetime, we backed out the laundry room, eyes still on the quartet. Didn't want to take our chances and get kidnapped. We left the laundry pirates, who were definitely letting their stiff denim and faux leather cowboy boots ruin the machine, to head back to the front of the store. We found Grandpa James circling the store with a coffee in hand. He sucked his teeth as soon as he saw me.

"Where you been? Huh? Come on, let's go."

Mikey and I followed behind Grandpa James to the counter to buy the sodas and snacks we were holding. And standing there in front of us was magic—we almost forgot! The holy grail that was going to teach me all the secrets to making it in Hollywood: the *Weekly World News*. I took one of the magazines down from the stand, read the tag for one of the stories, "Alien Bible Found! They Worship Oprah," and asked Grandpa if he'd buy it for me.

Taking it out of my hands, he said "Boy, no," but then he slowly flipped through the pages and slyly tossed the trash-azine on the counter with his other stuff. Mikey nudged me and nodded. We were so close. My fingers still smelled like the waxy, thin, ink-filled pages of the tabloid. Pages filled with stories of Morgan Freeman's favorite vocal cord massager, Demi Moore's organic Guatemalan-grown baby-stone-fruit juice cleanse, and Wesley Snipes's nonstop 48-hour one-on-one Tae Bo workout with Billy Blanks. Secrets to everlasting fame, a step-by-step blueprint for how to become a star.

We piled in the car and while my grandpa drove, I reached my hand in the bag and pulled out the magazine. It was shrouded in a golden glow. It felt magical. It felt forbidden. It felt holy. Mikey and I sat in the back seat and for the forty-five-minute drive back into town, we were captivated by every word on every page. There were stories of aliens, extreme weight loss, drunken nights on the town, secret societies, secret children, hideaway houses, and so much more. Mikey knew this was going to be my ticket to the big leagues. He made me study everything, and then he quizzed me.

"What are you going to do after you win your first Nickelodeon Award?"

"Adopt a lizard baby like the *Enquirer* said Hillary Clinton did."

"Which club do you not want to join?"

"The twenty-seven club."

From then on, every time we'd go into a store with Grandpa James, I'd read off one of the scandalous stories on the cover and he'd turn and say, "Lemme see that." And as he'd start telling me, "You too young to be—" he'd get distracted and mumble one of the other salacious story headlines to himself. My grandpa loved reading tabloids, and he loved a good conspiracy theory. He knew about aliens before anybody else. He knew where Hoffa was buried. He knew why they really kicked Pete Rose out of baseball.

Grandpa James never once complained about driving. He had a lot of opinions about how other people drove. Trust. But he got up every day, smoked a cigarette, coffee in hand, ate breakfast, read a tabloid, tossed on a hat, and got on the road. And when he wasn't on the road for work, he was still driving to truck stops. He was a creature of habit. He found freedom in his routine. There was absolutely nothing in those magazines for Mikey and me to learn from, but there was everything to be soaked up from Grandpa James.

He was one of my first mentors. The routine Grandpa James made for himself offered the same kind of comfort the routine of watching movies or reading did for me. And with repetition, I felt I had a chance of mastering my dreams, which gave me comfort.

Today, I love routine. I'm a habit-driven person. I find more freedom and creativity in routine than out of routine. And along the way, I found more mentors. They were all around me, whether I or they knew it or not; the forever student in me soaked up everything he could from so many of my family members, friends, teachers, etc., no matter how grand or mundane. Be it morning workouts, long drives to clear my mind, reading before bed—everything has been adopted from people in my life whom I admire and who have had an impact on who I've become. Role models.

PEER PRESSURED

"Why you in here, blood?"

THE FIRST COUPLE YEARS THAT MIKEY WAS IN AND OUT OF MY life were a rocky time. The same world that I had come to moderately understand and navigate felt different. I was just on the precipice of entering my teen years; internally my body was engaging in a warfare called puberty, and externally the social rules around me were ever-changing. There were times when I felt grounded and in control, and others when I was starved for Mikey's full-time guidance—or any guidance, really. This led me down the path of kicking it with other kids who, like me, had the superpower of getting in trouble.

We were loud in the cafeteria, we were late to class, and we pressured each other into doing childish stuff for no reason. It was fun. With a little more awareness of the world and hormones starting to send us all through voice cracks and bumpy skin, we were trying to find our way, and we all needed or were looking for something to ground us.

—

IN EIGHTH GRADE, AT A NEW SCHOOL YET AGAIN, I STUMBLED UPON three new friends who would become a part of the KRU, our high school clique, and who would also, to this day—along with Juan, aka 21 Questions (because there's not a question on God's green earth he hasn't asked); Malachi, aka Shallis (the self-crowned Prince of Magnet Charter Academy); Jesse, the old man; Vernon, shortened to V; and Joe, aka Bojang—be some of my closest friends. For eighth grade, though, these three new friends—Jason, Will, and Joseph—were my dawgs.

From the day I met him, Jason, also known as Pistol because he could shoot, always had plans to play basketball in college and then professionally. Nothing was going to stand in his way of doing so. He had a level of dedication that I had never seen before. It was uncanny; I wanted to soak it up. And because ball was life, he wouldn't do anything to jeopardize stepping on the court.

Will lived with his mom, Ms. Pat—who rocked a finger wave like Toni Braxton's hairdresser lived at her house—and stepdad, Bobby, who played the drums at our church and drove the first Mustang 5.0 I ever saw in person. They lived in the same apartment complex as I did, so I saw Will all of the time. He was a little shorter than me, had a bean-shaped head, could crack a joke on cue without thinking, and was a fast runner. He loved sports, mainly football. And his loyalty to his teammates and friends reminded me of Mikey. One of Will's closest friends was Fluzz, the quarterback of the football team, who lived one neighborhood over from Joe.

Joe was the wild card in the group. He was a bad boy

through and through. Everybody got the business. Teachers, classmates, and parents of classmates—no discrimination. I loved that about Joe. He never backed down. Not in school, not on the football field, and not in social situations. There was a fearlessness he had that I wanted. He always moved with zero fucks to give. And that freedom of moving through the world was enticing.

The four of us were always together at school. And when we talked about our weekend plans, it included all of us, except Jason because he was usually shooting in the gym every Saturday and Sunday. One Friday at lunch, Will, accompanied by Fluzz, plopped down at the table and said that his plan for Saturday was to spend the night at Fluzz's house. Fluzz was okay, but not my type of dude. He reeked of entitlement and mediocrity, but everything around him constantly reinforced the false message that he was a gift to the world. Therefore, when Will made his declaration, I knew I wasn't trying to be there. Neither was Joe. But when Fluzz said his single-parent mom had to work overnight and we'd be home solo, both Joe and I had a change of mind. No parents, no supervision? Yes. Please.

"You wanna stay at my house and we can walk over there?" Joe asked with one eyebrow raised. The same eyebrow he had his barber carve two slits in, to amplify his Big Daddy Kane–esque bad boy persona. I turned to Joe and casually threw out, "Yeah. I'll come over." Fluzz, who had already started drinking alcohol by this point—we were thirteen—immediately tossed out his proposed itinerary.

"I'll hide some of my mom's drank and we can drink and play PlayStation all night." Other than my dad and uncles giving me a few sips of beer every now and then, I had never really drank, but the plan was simple and attractive enough.

"I'm down."

Just then Meghan and her boyfriend, Andrew—another disciple of Fluzz's false Chosen One prophecy—walked by our table. He was holding her lunch tray, and she was bouncing in step with a few of her cheerleader friends.

"Look at this fucking clown," Will said, laughing. "She got his nose wide open." We laughed because it was true. Joe turned back to the table. Voice low. Looking serious, like Tom Cruise diffusing a bomb in a Mission: Impossible movie.

"Aye, don't she live by you?" he said in Fluzz's direction.

"Yeah, like two streets over."

A smile spread across Joe's face. "We should toilet paper her house." For a second only the noises of lunch trays banging on tables and silverware scraping plates filled the cavernous yellow-tiled cafeteria. Jason was the first to break the silence.

"Shooooot, mane, I'm out. I gotta go get up shots at the gym." The rest of us very quickly said we were not only down, but we got riled up too. We had no idea we were hype, but one by one we followed after each other.

"Yep."

"Hell yeah."

"'Bout to paper the shit outta her house."

"Let's get it."

With the four of us in agreement, the plan for the weekend was set.

THE NEXT NIGHT, WE WAITED UNTIL JOE'S MOM FELL ASLEEP. Once the coast was clear, we tiptoed our way into the kitchen, where his mom kept all the house supplies. Joe and I each grabbed a twelve-pack of toilet paper—thanking Sam's Club for the bulk—and moved back to Joe's room. The door to Joe's mom's room was shut. So he wasn't worried about her waking up and catching us. He was worried about his little sister, Andrea, waking up and snitching. Joe grabbed a can of WD-40 from under his bed and walked over to the window. He meticulously sprayed the sides of the single-pane metal-framed window, making sure he didn't miss a single spot.

"What you doing?" I whispered.

"Making sure the window don't make noise and wake my sister up." Never taking his eyes off the mission. Joe had clearly done this before. I had never snuck out of my parents' house, not that I didn't try. I did. A lot. But my problem was everywhere we lived, they always turned the alarm on at night or they'd booby-trap the doors and windows of the apartment so nobody could get *in*. Which also meant I couldn't get *out*.

Joe raised the oiled window up without a sound. We threw the toilet paper out the window and shimmied out. Feet on the ground, we took off running.

Joe and I stealthily wound our way through the neighborhood of modest ranch-style houses. We jumped a chain-link fence and found ourselves on the sprawling unkempt yard of our rival middle school. Joe and I both didn't actually go to the school we were supposed to attend. Both our parents bused us to Byrd Middle School because it had more resources. At the time, there was no equal distribution of tax dollars to every school.

We walked across the Alice in Wonderland–themed school grounds, never breaking stride. We had to get across the school's field, walk through the parking lot, and then cross a busy street with two lanes on each side to get to the outer edge of Fluzz's neighborhood. From there, we just needed to walk a few streets over and about halfway up the block, and we'd be drinking and toilet papering all night long.

Once we made it to Fluzz's house, it was like we had fallen down a rabbit hole. As soon as we stepped through the front door, we were hit with a stomach-curdling malodor. The floor was littered with shoes, tossed and discarded like shells at a crab boil. The boys were in the living room, where they were already drinking and playing video games. Spread out on the coffee table were a few mostly eaten pizzas. Holding game controller #1, Fluzz had a strong buzz going for himself, and although Will said he was only one drink in, he seemed frat-boy wasted. The thing that threw Joe and me, though, was the person holding game controller #2: Andrew—Meghan's sheepdog boyfriend. No drink in his hand, and a preppy light orange polo buttoned to the top.

Andrew on his best day was mayonnaise. And I know I'm talking about an eighth-grade kid, but using that same eighth-grade perspective, he was mayonnaise. He gave off an odd energy. He always tucked in his shirts. His hair was cut for a seventy-three-year-old banker. And he moved with the caution and fear of the most conservative accountant during tax season. He was also Fluzz's full-time yes-man, which perfectly suited Fluzz's self-infatuation. If he were underwear, he'd be tighty-whities.

"When we going to do this?" Will asked the group with a slight slur. His Midwestern drawl thick like molasses from the liquor.

"After this game," Fluzz mumbled, eyes concentrated on the screen.

"What are you guys talking about?" Andrew asked. He had given over his controller to Joe. Apparently Fluzz hadn't informed him about the mission we'd hatched the day before.

"We're going toilet papering," I said. Andrew had a slight flinch in his eyes, a glitch in the matrix.

"Toilet what? I don't think that's a good idea. What if you get caught?" Andrew squawked.

"Stop being a bitch, Drew. We're just gonna go and come back." Fluzz lashed out like a thirty-year career drunk hunched over a bar at last call. And thank God, because it shut Andrew down. Which saved Joe, Will, and me from having to have a drawn-out existential conversation on toilet papering and the risk factors involved.

"Fuck!" Joe yelled. On the TV, Fluzz had just scored again as the clock ran out in the fourth quarter of their *Madden '96* game.

Fluzz stood up, pounded his drink, then pounded his chest. "Somebody stop me!" Imitating Jim Carrey from *The Mask*. "Let's do this shit, dude!" And with that we loaded up our supplies and headed out the door.

THE WALK FROM FLUZZ'S HOUSE TO MEGHAN'S HOUSE WAS RELA-tively short. Maybe seven minutes of weaving and wandering through the master-planned tree-lined neighborhood streets. Everyone except Andrew carried toilet paper. For three teen-age boys impaired by vodka and tequila, we were pretty quiet as we covertly moved through the neighborhood.

"Meghan lives on this street," Andrew said, as we cut right down a block. A sly grin slid across my face.

We stopped a bit before we approached Meghan's house.

Andrew, unaware we weren't still walking, took a few more steps down the street.

"Dude, what are you doing? We're here," Fluzz said. Andrew turned and looked back in our direction. He gingerly returned to the group.

"Guys, this is Meghan's house." He whispered like the feds were listening. Will was the only one to acknowledge him.

"Yeah, we know."

"Dude, she's my girlfriend. I can't toilet paper her house."

Joe started laughing. "Just 'cause she let you hold her lunch tray don't mean shit. I bet you ain't even hit it yet." Andrew shrank. He had not had sex with Meghan or with anyone. None of us had.

"Yeah, you ain't even got to touch it."

"Nah, he ain't got his dick wet." Teenage boys will be teenage boys. Posturing at its best.

Meghan's house looked like it had been ripped out of a magazine, like it was one of the houses in *Melrose Place*. It was white with a tall, brown-shingled roof. The windows across the front were wide and inviting with flowy white curtains that framed the sides. There was a brick path that curled its way around a giant tree before stopping at the WELCOME HOME doormat that lay in front of the door. Tiny beautiful spots of light floated through the giant tree in the front yard like fairies. For a few moments, we all took in the house. Nothing like what any of us had lived in, except Andrew. And although Fluzz and Meghan technically lived in the same neighborhood, it changed quite a bit from the older, developed periphery to the newer-built center.

"Guys—"

Before Andrew could finish his final plea, Fluzz ripped

open his toilet paper and ran. And with Andrew watching, the other three of us followed, each with a twelve-pack of toilet paper. Forty-eight rolls of Charmin's softest double-ply. We tossed rolls over the tree at, and to, each other. Fluzz threw a Hail Mary pass. Will used his extremely fast feet to run circles around the tree, wrapping the trunk in layers of the cotton munitions. When we first started, we giggled like kids passing notes in class. But about halfway through, the alcohol and serotonin kicked in and we were cackling loud, like my malt liquor–drinking uncles around a domino table. Andrew never moved. He just watched. Nervously scanning to see if anyone was coming.

"There's a light!" he yelled. We all froze and contorted left and right to see what he saw. A neighbor across the street had turned on a light inside their living room. No one asked questions, we just ran. Will led the way, and after a few long minutes of all-out sprinting we were back on the far end of Fluzz's street. Gassed and sucking for air, we all dropped our hands to our knees. The only sound was our lungs vacuuming all the cold night air they could, and then I busted out in a laugh. Then Joe. Then Fluzz. Then Will. Andrew did not. Mayonnaise. After a few seconds of laughing at what we had just done, relieved we'd escaped our brush with getting caught, the laughter started to taper.

"Shit," Fluzz said quietly, looking in the direction of his driveway. We all turned. Fluzz, deflated, said, "My mom's home."

We all knew what that meant for Fluzz. That house was a disaster when we left. And with empty alcohol bottles sitting around, he was about to be in it. Unfortunately for Will and Andrew, they had to go through that experience with him because they were spending the night there. But Joe and I were not going in there.

Because we got interrupted at Meghan's house, we didn't actually use all of the toilet paper we had brought. And because Fluzz was about to get busted, he didn't want to take the leftovers into his house and have to explain to his mom why he was walking around drunk with rolls of toilet paper in the middle of the night. So, Joe and I took the leftover rolls, stuffed them under our Starter jackets, and bid farewell to Fluzz, Will, and Andrew before making our journey back to Joe's.

WE TOOK THE SAME ROUTE THAT WE HAD TAKEN TO FLUZZ'S house to get back to Joe's. We walked at a quick pace. I had a bounce in my step. The rush of almost getting caught coursed through my veins.

"That shit was crazy! If we got caught, I woulda been out," I said, laughing. Joe chimed in with a chuckle.

"You see the look on Andrew's ol' square-ass face? That boy gotta change his tighty-whities tonight. Yessir."

As we approached the four-lane busy street, I looked left and right. A few cars were traveling in each direction.

"Hol' up. Let these cars pass," I said. Joe nodded in agreement. And as soon as they passed, we ran across the street laughing and yelling. Only one car was coming toward us now. It zoomed past us as we crossed into the far lane and stepped onto the grounds of our rival middle school.

"Bruh, Fluzz 'bout to be in trouble, ain't he?" I asked. "Drunk and sneaking out. If she find out he toilet papered that house, he ain't 'bout to see a football for a year."

Joe started laughing again. "His momma 'bout to bring the belt out on his ass, ahahahaha." Why that was funny, I have no idea. We had been conditioned to laugh at somebody when they got in trouble—even though, through our own experience, we should have learned to show some care and compassion.

Whooop, whoooooooop! The sounds of an approaching siren broke our laughter. We both turned to make sure it wasn't behind us, but our dreams were quickly crushed. It was. A cop car quickly revved all of its publicly funded Crown Victoria engine into the parking lot of the middle school, and as it approached, we became framed and blinded by the cold white rays of a spotlight. Joe and I both froze like we had stared Medusa in the eyes. We knew better than to run. We knew better than to do anything but just stand there.

The officer climbed out, making the car rock from side to side. He approached with his hands on his hips, ready.

"What you boys doing?" he asked.

Joe defiantly stared him in the eyes. "Walking home."

"This late? You know it's a curfew? How old are y'all?"

"We old enough," Joe trumpeted. Without moving my head, I cut my eyes toward him. I usually loved Joe's cavalierness toward authority, but at this moment, I did not.

"We're thirteen," I said, to cut the awkward beat.

The officer huffed. "Then you should have been home three hours ago. Curfew is ten if you're under fifteen," he said.

"Well, we close to my house. It's just right there," said Joe.

"Won't matter now. I'm gonna have to take y'all to juvenile—" A roll of toilet paper fell from under my Sonics Starter jacket. It rolled for about ten feet before it hit a curb and stopped.

"You boys carrying toilet paper?" the officer asked. Joe and I both nodded.

"How much?"

Neither of us knew exactly. So we slowly opened our jackets and let the toilet paper fall to the ground. The officer, amused, chuckled to himself.

"You two go to this school?"

"No"/"Nope," we said.

Joe stood proudly. "We go to Byrd."

The officer looked at us and then at the rolls of toilet paper that lay on the asphalt. He looked at the time on his watch. It was close to two in the morning.

"I don't really feel like driving downtown. So you boys pick up the paper and I'll take you home." One by one, with the officer watching over us, we picked up the rolls that had dropped from our jackets.

When we got to Joe's house, the officer banged on the door like a landlord looking for late rent. Joe's mom, who had been asleep, stumbled to the door and pulled the curtain back. She saw Joe and me standing there with the officer and was immediately snapped out of her sleep state. She quickly popped the door open. The officer told her that we had broken curfew. She was dumbfounded. She didn't know how we had snuck out of the house. The officer then told her that he caught us trying to toilet paper the nearby middle school. He finished by telling her that with all we had done, with "intent" and "breaking curfew," he would have to write a citation for it, and we would have to go to court. As his words rambled on, I could feel the ancestors gathering around me to take my soul after my parents killed me.

The next day, Joe's mom drove me home. There was silence in the car the whole way. The hum of the engine was the only soundscape to my inner monologue hypothesizing my parents' reaction. When we got to my house, Joe's mom made Joe come to the door as well. She rang the doorbell and my dad answered. She told him everything that had happened the night before. At least what she knew. She apologized that we had gotten in trouble. She then made Joe apologize to my dad for us sneaking out. My dad didn't say much. He was hard to read. But I went inside knowing I was grounded.

A FEW WEEKS LATER, MY DAD DROVE ME DOWN TO THE TULSA courthouse for my hearing date. We moved through the oppressive, drab, low-lit hallways and found the sterile, soul-robbing courtroom we were assigned to. Sitting high on his throne of butterflied mahogany was a judge in his mid-to-late sixties, with thin hair and sunken eyes. We waited as each case went up, one by one, all for different things. There were adults who had evaded police. There were people who had broken their probation. Folks were there for bench warrants for speeding tickets. It was a melting pot of offenses and collateral consequences. An hour and a half in, the judge called my name.

Dressed in my Sunday clothes, I approached the defendants' table. From all of the courtroom shows of the time, I was sure I was going to have to enter a plea, but it didn't work out that way. The judge did all of the talking. He read out a statement from the officer and the notes on the citation, and then stopped.

"Are your parents here?" he asked. I nodded.

"Yes, my dad," and I turned and pointed. The judge narrowed his eyes and looked at my dad.

"Mr. Ellis, can you stand next to your son, please?" he "asked." My dad stepped over a few people and joined me at the defendants' table. The judge told my dad that he was responsible for my behavior and that he needed to do a better job of raising his child. He questioned whether my parents were fit to parent if I was running around toilet papering a school after curfew. And lastly, he told my dad he should be ashamed of himself for "not doing a better job of keeping control" of me. The judge gave me twenty hours of community service and told my dad next time it would be him who got sentenced, and he wouldn't be as lenient.

After the judge berated him, my dad was hotter than fish grease at a Juneteenth block party in Texas. He didn't talk the whole way home from the courthouse. Judging by the fury built up behind his eyes, I knew my boys would be rapping "When they reminisce over you, my God" by the end of the day. During that silent ride home, I began to realize that what I had done directly affected my parents. I represented my parents. And everything I did, regardless of whether it deserved a ridiculous, humiliating, and coded lecture or not was in some way a reflection of them. When I do good, they do good. When I do bad, they do bad. We were forever linked in that way. My actions had ripple effects in their lives as well. That realization/burden is a lot for a teenage kid to carry. Especially an only child. But I never wanted to see something like the anger and shame my dad held happen to them because of something I did ever again. I would definitely do something stupid again, multiple more times, for various reasons—probably even still today—but at that moment, with a judgment staring me and my dad down, I was at least made aware of it.

—

A FEW WEEKS AFTER THE GREAT TOILET PAPER CAPER, MY MIDDLE school was privy to my run-in with the court system. I found myself constantly under the strongest of microscope lenses. Teachers and administrators looked at me with suspicion; I could sense their concern for their, and perhaps other students', safety. Joe and I had truly been branded as "the bad kids." Therefore, we were perfect for a new program that included a field trip.

The security guard at our school was in charge of hand-picking kids to go to "Big Mac," McAlester maximum security prison, to do a Scared Straight trip. Yes, it's exactly what you're thinking. Just like the MTV show. Joe and I, along with seven other kids, were chosen to go, as long as the security guard got approval from a parent or guardian. Conveniently, this same security guard—who thought he was funny like Martin Lawrence playing Otis—was also always trying to holler at my mom.

The security guard—to borrow from the third installment of the classic film franchise *Friday*, let's call him Top Flight Security—called each student's house one by one, and explained why he wanted to take each kid. The first two times he called my house, he got the answering machine—thanks to my parents' new, upwardly mobile jobs at the bank office and the airplane hangar, respectively—allowing me to intercept the call.

After getting in trouble a few times earlier in the school year, I noticed the principal would always leave a message on the answering machine, which is how my parents were first tipped off to my behavioral issues at school. After some trial and error, I learned how to erase the messages. The first two times Top Flight Security called, I blitzed the answering machine; if I kept it up for one or two more days, I'd be in the clear. What I couldn't play my Deion Sanders level of dominant defense on was an in-person run-in.

"You gon' miss the bus. You betta hurry up!" my mom yelled from the kitchen as I stood in the mirror making sure the crease in my new jeans lay right. Every day, I spent more than half my morning religiously watching Stuart Scott flipping puns on *SportsCenter* and impulsively running my arm back and forth, iron in hand, over my jeans. And just to make sure I was extra smooth, I had a full stock of extra-stiff starch at all times. My routine was fueled by my forever goal to have Brandy and Monica in battling duet hollering "The boy is mine!" when I graced the halls. This morning, my routine was the exact same, except I somehow managed to put a double crease in my jeans, making me miss the bus.

I burst through the front door and ran to the bus stop—not too fast, because I didn't want to mess up my fit. As soon as I turned the corner and lay eyes on the stop, the doors were closing and the bus putted away, leaving a trail of black smoke behind.

"I told you you were going to miss the bus. Come on, let's go. I don't have time." My mom was just backing out when I got to the house; she had rolled her window down and cut her eyes.

I carefully dropped into the passenger seat and shut the door. The automatic seatbelt sprang into action, but I reached up quickly and disconnected it.

"Boy, put that seatbelt on." I huffed. I puffed. And I plugged the seatbelt back in, but for the ride to school I held it away from my body so it wouldn't touch my perfectly pressed shirt.

Since I missed the bus, I ended up getting to school late. And since I was late, my mom had to come into the building and sign me in with the registrar. We were walking toward the front doors when someone called out.

"Ms. Paula, that you?" echoed from behind us. We both turned. My mom sighed and my eyes widened.

"Yeah, I thought I recognized you from the back," Top Flight said.

Bruh, chill. That's my moms.

"Hi. Yeah. Wendell was running late this morning, so I had to bring him," my mom said through a forced smile.

"Okay . . . okay. I tried calling you a few times"—my mom's face scrunched—"about the field trip. Did you get my messages?"

"No. When did you call? What field trip?" she asked.

"I called you twice this week. I'm taking the boys over to McAlester to have an ol' powwow with some of the inmates. Just to learn how they got there, and teach our boys to stay outta trouble." The calculus my mom did in those eight seconds was worthy of a position at NASA.

"You called twice this week and left messages? I check the machine every night when I get home. It's been empty all week." She looked at me as she spoke with a knowing glare. "Yes, he can go on the field trip. Might teach him something." My shoulders folded in on themselves, as Top Flight got excited.

"Okay now, I'll send a slip home for him to sign today. It has my number on it, so if you ever need anything or wanna talk, you can call me," he said with a smile.

"I'll have my husband call if we have any questions." Now his shoulders folded. Not only had his dreams been stomped out like Kirk Franklin and the Family singing on a Sunday, but now he was stuck with me. My mom turned toward the office, and I followed. I tossed my head up to the sky and gave the biggest eye roll and groan that those middle school halls had ever seen.

Four days later I stood in the blinding morning sun, waiting with the rest of my Scared Straight group for our bus to take us on the field trip from hell. We could hear the squeal and squeak of the bus before it even turned the corner. It abruptly jerked to a stop in front of us, and the nine of us with Top Flight Security—who actually kind of looked like Mark Curry but couldn't hoop like Mark Curry—climbed onto the big empty yellow bus. We spread out, taking up as much room as we could. None of us knew what to expect in terms of what our day was going to be like, but a few people used their limited experience with visiting prison to make guesses.

"When we went to see my cousin in Alford last year, we had to go through like three metal detectors and four big-ass gates."

"We took a bunch of stuff to my brother, and the guards tore through everything before he could have it."

"These bamas bet not try to strip-search us or I'ma bust one of 'em in they head."

"Ayeeeee, you lying. You like that shit."

"Shut the fuck up."

"Come shut me—"

"Both y'all asses shut up 'fore I come back there," Top Flight yelled. The bus quieted.

"Blahahaha, yo' rent-a-cop ass ain't gon' do shit."

All nine of us erupted into laughter.

WHEN WE PULLED THROUGH THE GIANT WHITE OKLAHOMA STATE Penitentiary arch, and past the guard shack at the prison entrance, it began to feel like Shawshank without the redemption. Everyone was tense. Top Flight gave us four rules to follow while inside Big Mac: only speak when spoken to, do not look any of the inmates in the eye, keep your hands out of your pockets, and stay with the group. He also informed us that we'd all have to take our street clothes off because of gang-affiliated colors, and wear the same prison-issued jumpsuit the inmates wore.

"Aww, hell nah, mane, I ain't wearing no prison jumpsuit. You got me bent," one boy yelled from behind me. My mind was racing. I'd had brushes with colors before. But those were in a school and a movie theater. This was different. These were dudes who were for real, got locked up for banging, and now we were in prison with them.

"Say bruh, why we even here? Ain't none of us in prison," a kid toward the middle of the bus asked. Top Flight reached into his diaphragm and brought out the deepest tonal chord that he could hit.

"This is to teach y'all that all the trouble you getting into ain't gonna lead you but one place, and that's right here. So, you can see what your life is about to be like. Now let's go." And with that, the bus stopped and one by one we clopped, tromped, and mean-mugged our way toward the front doors of Big Mac. Right inside the entry were five guards, a standing metal detector, a bag scanner, and a bulletproof glass window with another guard sitting inside the safety of the glass. The room was bare, save for signage in black and red bold caps that listed out visitation rules.

We emptied our pockets and went through the metal detector. The machine beeped as some of the boys crossed through the threshold. They had to spread their arms and legs for a very aggressive and intimate pat-down by two officers. After watching a few of my comrades pass through unscathed and a few get the pat-down, I stammer-stepped my way through and, luckily, was all good. We were ushered through a gate that was opened by the guard beyond the bulletproof glass, and on the other side of the doors we were met by a guard, a case manager, and an inmate: Dino.

Dino was about twenty-five years old. He stood a little taller than most of us, probably six-one, and was fully tatted. There wasn't a clear space of skin anywhere but around his eyes. He was the living embodiment of someone we had all emulated in our movement or speech at one time or another, in an attempt to act hard. Dino was also a Blood—and even though he was doing a life bid and it didn't matter anymore, he still hadn't turned his back on that commitment he made—he still repped his set.

Upon meeting us, Dino didn't say anything. He barely even acknowledged us, but he stayed with the group as a docent to our prison-guided tour—even into the inmate bathrooms, where we each had to strip down to our underwear and put on our oversized Oklahoma corrections uniforms.

"Don't drop the soap, nigga!" one of the boys yelled out. "Ahahahahha." His childish joke bouncing off the tiled walls of the vapid space. It broke most of our nervousness and there were a few chuckles from the group. Dino, still, just watched us.

"Alright, thas enuff. You boys drop your civilians ova here an' line up," the prison guard yelled. After that, we were cuffed like a chain gang around our ankles and wrists and dragged through the grounds of the prison like a plowing horse being pulled through a field. Our HGTV-style prison tour started with sightseeing the different cells in various blocks within the general population. Inmates, who mostly looked like us, were all around, some staring at us; others barely noticed.

From there, we were taken into a solitary confinement cell. It was so tiny, only two of us could go in at a time. We were then paraded through the cafeteria, during lunchtime, which was in full swing. We stood in line with the inmates to order our food, and with trays in hand we walked to an open table while folks laughed, commented, and catcalled us like we were being escorted onto a chopping block. Guards stood watch, every few feet. Overseeing. We dropped at our lunch table and quietly ate. None of us were anywhere near intellectually equipped or emotionally aware to understand what was happening to us. So, to hide the nerves and anxiety that crawled over our skin and rattled through our brains, we made more jokes.

We finished our cold meal in the cafeteria, and we were taken into a large multipurpose room with two rows of chairs lined up. Ankle by ankle and wrist by wrist, we were uncuffed and told to sit. Before we could even sit back in the seats, Dino went in.

"Why y'all lil niggas in here?" he said in a low, gravelly grunt. No one spoke up.

"You," he pointed to the first kid in the row. One by one he went down the aisle making us each tell him why we were chosen by Top Flight Security to come to this horrible school-sanctioned prevention program.

"I dunno," shrugged one kid.

Dino didn't like the unknown. His tone shifted. "Oh, you don't know, huh? When you get in here and you some nigga's bitch, you gon' know then?" A few of us snickered but he only caught one, Mike.

"You think that shit funny?" he asked Mike. Mike's big white teeth flashed through a confident, unaffected smile and he nodded.

"What's your name?"

"Mike."

"And why you in here, Mike?"

"I guess I be getting in trouble and shit," Mike casually tossed out. "Plus they be on me 'cause I'm a Crip." No one spoke. Dino put his hands folded together in front of him.

"Come up here, Mike," he said. A quizzical look spread across Mike's face that read, *Who, me?* And even though the question was unspoken, Dino answered.

"Yes you, nigga! Get the fuck up here."

Mike chuckled and obliged. He stood next to Dino. Didn't flinch. Didn't look away. He was defiant. His body language screaming with the bass of Master P's voice, *I'm 'bout it, 'bout it.* Dino sensed it.

"Since you so hard, I'm 'bout to make you my bitch today," Dino said as he reached his hand into his pocket. Mike smiled.

"Whatever, bruh."

Dino pulled his pocket inside out, and like the endless clips you can see on YouTube, he told Mike to hold his pocket. I looked at Mike, then Dino, and then slowly scanned over everyone else in the room. Were we all witnessing the same thing? Is Top Flight going to step in and break this up? Why the hell am I here? Over some toilet paper?

Mike didn't move to hold the pocket. Instead he laughed. "I ain't doing that shit."

Dino leaned into Mike's ear and whispered. Mike didn't budge. A few seconds into the sweet nothings Dino was whispering to Mike, his body language completely changed. His eyes pointed to the ground and didn't make contact with anyone. The hot air in his chest slowly leaked out of his body as his expression changed from a smile to one of concern. We never heard what Dino said, but Mike reached for his pocket and held it as Dino moved around the room and questioned the rest of us, Mike following closely behind.

Dino interrogated four people after he broke Mike, before he got to me. From the line of questioning of everyone in front of me, I knew his first question was going to be *Why are you here?* But I didn't really have an answer. I didn't know. Sure, I had been late to a few classes, and got in trouble breaking curfew, but could that really have been the reason I was bused to meet Dino? I knew plenty of other kids at school who had also been in as much trouble, if not more, and none of them had been invited on this cultural tour of Big Mac.

"Why you in here, blood?" Dino asked, Mike in tow.

"I got in trouble for breaking curfew and toilet papering somebody house with some friends."

"Yo' friends get in trouble too?"

"Yeah."

"Whose idea it was?" he probed. I wasn't expecting that. He wanted me to snitch on Joe, who was right next to me. I could sense Joe's eyes pleading with me not to say anything, but I wasn't looking away from Dino after the Mike incident. I wasn't holding a pocket.

"Uh, it was—I mean—we all kinda came up with it," I said.

"So, you put pressure on somebody to do it or they pressure you?" I wasn't really sure how to answer. Either I was the instigator, which wasn't true, or I was a snitch, which I didn't want to be. Luckily it didn't matter. Dino turned to the whole group.

"What y'all lil niggas need to learn is peer pressure is what's going to get you locked up in here with a bunch of goons who don't give a fuck. You running around doing stupid shit being pressed by your homeys, and catch a case, you gon' be right here with me. Ain't no calling Mommy when you holding somebody pocket every day." He paused, and then nodded for Mike to take his seat.

Dino told us his journey to being locked up. He joined a gang when he was fourteen, and from there he started stealing and fighting. He said he later started selling drugs because all his boys were. It's what they did. And that gradually led to more and more fights with other rival gangs. One night, he and his boys were partying and some other gang did a drive-by on them. Dino busted back, and ended up killing one of the guys. He said the police found him hiding under his grandmother's house a week later. He had been at Big Mac ever since.

At the end of our time with Dino, we were escorted back to the changing rooms and given our clothes. Everyone was quiet. The jokes had all gone away. We went back through the complex gate system, watching as the heavy steel-bar door shut in Dino's face.

I'M NOT SURE OUR TRIP TO BIG MAC WAS AS DETERRING AS TOP Flight or the administrators at our school would have hoped. For the first few weeks we all stayed out of trouble, but after some time, we all ended up ourselves again. None of us, that I know of, went to jail. But none of us were ever meant to go to jail. None of us were ever going down that path. We just were rambunctious kids who went to school in an environment where our administrators treated and punished us differently than our counterparts who had the same behavior, or worse. We time-jumped from boys to men at that school, and none of us knew it then. I now fully realize Dino was in character, trying to scare the shit out of us in order to keep us out of trouble—not exactly the best way to deal with kids acting out. I didn't need to learn the lesson of "Don't go to jail" in any other way, but for years I have remembered Dino's speech about peer pressure, as much as I have remembered the judgment my teachers, administrators, and school staff—like Top Flight—showed me and my friends. If it were up to them, I would have been pressured into believing I was less than and that my fate was sealed. I'm grateful that wasn't the case.

"The. Bayou. Classic! Bruh, are you Black?"

BOOKER T. WASHINGTON HIGH SCHOOL WAS TULSA PUBLIC Schools' only magnet high school in the city when I was a kid. The campus sits on the north side of town, less than a mile from historic Greenwood, aka Black Wall Street. Being a magnet school meant it was the best education TPS had to offer students in the district. You had to apply to get in. Fifty percent of the student body were bused in—test scores and application–dependent—from all over Tulsa.

To be real, I'm not sure how I got into Booker T. My test scores were good but not great; I wasn't in all the activities in middle school; and my essay for the application centered on my dreams of playing basketball for the BTW Hornets. But when I got my acceptance letter in the mail, I didn't ask questions. I was going to be an "often imitated, never duplicated" Booker T. Washington Hornet.

BTW's halls were filled with primarily Black students, and everything about the school was fresher and better than at any other Tulsa school. The colors (orange and black), the outfits, the girls, the sports teams, the history—to be at Booker T. was "to be young, gifted, and Black." It was Black Excellence years before that term was coined.

BOOKER T. WASHINGTON floated proudly above the doors of the main entrance. During the Tulsa Race Massacre of 1921 the school had been used by the Red Cross as its headquarters for relief efforts to the people of North Tulsa. The school had won over forty state championships in various sports, was accredited by the International Baccalaureate Organization to grant college credits to students, and had one of the most famous high school marching bands in the country. EXCELLENCE in every way.

In my freshman year I oscillated between the basketball court—where past, present, and future NBA players Wayman Tisdale, Richard Dumas, Etan Thomas, and Ryan Humphrey all played legendary games—and the football field, where NFL names R. W. McQuarters, Robert Meachem, Kevin Lockett, Aaron Lockett, and Tyler Lockett (yes, they were all related) banged and twisted their way into state championships and NCAA scholarships. Unfortunately, I was not on the same athletics standout path as any of these phenoms. I didn't score 20 a game or punctuate a 30-point win with a windmill that would have Dick Vitale dub me "Skywalker." That was Ryan.

The band director, Mr. Daniels, was shorter than most of the students. He had a round belly and an Afro with gray streaks that reached to the sky like Don King's. He was as tough on the band as the head coaches were on their basketball and football teams, and he had been the band director at Booker T. for years. He was as respected and revered in the hallways as any staff member on campus.

The Booker T. band was known throughout Tulsa and the state as an aspirational band. Everyone knew that even if it was only during a twenty-minute halftime, the band was the main attraction even when a state championship–winning team, with multiple future NCAA players, was on the field. Their show was amazing. Coordinated colors, movement, sound, and song selection—Mr. Daniels made art. It was the band that created the slogan—which the school as a whole ultimately adopted—to contextualize Hornet band culture: "often imitated, never duplicated."

DEANDRE LITTLEJOHN AND I SPENT A YEAR OF SCHOOL TOGETHER in seventh grade. Because I joined that school at the top of the school year and had missed a few days, I wasn't able to pick my electives. I was stuck with German and band. When I heard the registrar tell this to my mom, I thought, *What in the hell am I going to do with that?* I had tried piano to be like Ray Charles, and took guitar lessons to be like Lenny Kravitz, but a combination of low funds and disinterest collided on the train track of puberty and I quit. I didn't know how to play a single instrument—what the hell was I going to do in band?

When I got to my first class, every student was warming up their fingers and lips. I sat still, watching, unsure of what to do. Amid the wafting teenage angst that floated above the cacophony of sounds, a recognizable piano riff broke through: Dr. Dre's "Nuthin' but a 'G' Thang."

At the piano was a chocolate-skinned, bean-headed kid with glasses thick enough to start a forest fire. Beanhead, also known as DeAndre, with no sheet music in front of him, was putting down one of hip-hop's greatest classics . . . on a piano. Without a doubt, he was one of the most talented musicians I had ever met in my life. I would later learn that he could play anything on a piano after listening to it just once or twice. He played by ear and had perfect pitch. I was in awe.

The band director quieted the band and, noticing me, the only kid without an instrument, assigned me the instrument he needed to complete the sound and range he was looking for. And so, within a few minutes of being in the real-life *Making the Band,* I had a giant-ass brass sousaphone placed around my neck.

A couple years later at Booker T., I had no intention whatsoever to join the band. I didn't care how bad and "known in the land" they were, I was there to hoop! I was happy watching the halftime show from the sidelines. And the band would be playing the score to my on-court runs. But when one of Mr. Daniels's sousaphone players moved away, he needed another. DeAndre, who had become the Nick Cannon of Booker T. on the all-upperclassman drumline, said he knew somebody. For the next few weeks Mr. Daniels and DeAndre chased me around the school trying to get me to join the band. I ducked and dodged these dudes for three or four weeks.

At the same time, I was struggling to fit into Hornet basketball. I would pop out instead of slash, I was cutting instead of sliding to the corner, and I was reaching instead of taking the charge. It wasn't that I was bad. I just didn't have the same feel for the team and the style of play that Coach wanted me to have. I felt like I was on the outside, and day after day, no matter how hard I tried, I felt more disenfranchised and less motivated.

Therefore, when DeAndre's feet shuffled across the cafeteria floor and he barked "Come with us to the Classic" to me, I caved. Right then, I needed to be needed, to be valuable for a team. I also had no idea what the Classic was. "What's classic?" I asked. DeAndre's eyes bugged out of his Steve Urkel–thick glasses. "The. Bayou. Classic! Bruh, are you Black?" The overly analytical voice in my mind raced: *What does me knowing what the Bayou Classic is have to do with my Blackness? Wait, is my Blackness in question with anybody else? DOES EVERYONE IN THIS SCHOOL KNOW WHAT THE BAYOU CLASSIC IS EXCEPT ME?*

"Ohhhh, THE Classic," I said to DeAndre. "Hell yeah, I know the Classic. I'm not stupid . . ." I studied his face, thinking he was going to call my bluff as he sat quiet and expressionless for a beat.

"Aight. Well, the band is going to the Battle of the Bands and you should come. Whoever wins gets to perform before the Classic at the Superdome, and Mr. Daniels wants you to come with us to check it out," he excitedly rattled off. I'm not sure DeAndre understood that my gangly and concerningly skinny body would be weighed down by a patinated brass sousaphone wrapped around my neck like a boa constrictor, while I played the Gap Band's "You Dropped a Bomb on Me" off-key, but it didn't matter because he was selling me like the homey on a corner selling CDs out of his trunk. I suddenly had to go to the Classic, and after the near abysmal reputation-destroying moment seconds earlier, when I didn't know what the Classic was, I didn't want to tempt the ancestors.

"That sound cool as hell. I'll go," I said as nonchalantly as I could, trying not to give away how desperate I was to not mess this up.

DeAndre nodded his head. "Bet!"

Two weeks later I stepped off the bus at the Southern University and A&M College football stadium, and immediately I was in heaven. There were about ten all-Black high school bands from all over the country scattered around. Majorettes twirled batons, drum majors stretched their legs as they commanded the field amid the mismatched sounds of percussion, brass, and woodwind players warming up their instruments.

Mr. Daniels stood a few feet away from the bus. He didn't say a word, but like soldiers preparing for a battle, everyone knew to gather around their leader. After the sixty or so kids settled, Mr. Daniels, with his raspy, distressed-vocal-cord voice, spoke up.

"Y'all know how hard we worked to get here. Today is about one thing and one thing only: being perfect in every single beat, moment, step, and note that we have worked on all year. The only way to get to tomorrow [playing on-field at the Bayou Classic at the Superdome] is to do what we need to do today." He paused for a minute, scanning the group. "I am so proud of you all. Now let's go swarm."

Everyone started clapping and yelling; the excitement was palpable. My heart raced. I started jumping up and down. These band nerds and ridiculously fine flag-bearers and majorettes had me hyped like I'd just listened to "Tear da Club Up" by Three 6 Mafia before running onto the court for a game.

On the field, the Hornet band didn't disappoint. They played the prearranged set that they played at halftime for the Booker T. football games. When they ended the set, every band in the stands stood still, eyes locked on the field. They all studied their competition. Looking at the Hornet band as if to say, *That's it?* Fans in the stands who came out for the battle cheered and screamed. On the field, the Hornet band stood still. Frozen. Not a single muscle twitched on anyone. It made the non-competitors in the crowd go even more wild. After about a minute or two the crowd began to quiet, and five members of the percussion section stepped forward and stood shoulder to shoulder, DeAndre leading the group.

Growing up in Tornado Alley, you learn the signs of impending destruction headed your way. Just before the funnel cloud of a tornado forms, everything in the natural world slows and quiets. Winds stop blowing and animals go into hiding. You can hear a pin drop from miles away. It is eerie AF. And then, in a split second, just when the unnerving quiet gets under your skin and makes every hair on your body stand up, all hell breaks loose. The funnel cloud comes down and destroys everything in its path. That unnerving calm that ultimately became scorched earth was the drumline at Booker T. Washington High School.

The five drummers waited until the crowd was dead silent, and then they went IN. They played an arrangement of "Ride with Me" by Nelly and yelled out "Oh, oh oh" with the song. They flipped their drumsticks in perfect synchronicity, they played the drum of the person to their left and then their right, never missing a beat. Every time the chorus came around, the entire band would scream "MUST BE THE MONEY!" And the crowd in the stands went crazy. People started bouncing their heads and throwing their hands up as if they were tossing money in the air. It was a dance party in the stands. The drummers lifted their left legs and raised their right arms up. Standing on one leg, they played with the arm opposite the raised leg. When their feet came crashing to the ground it was in perfect unison and a *BOOM!* rumbled through the field. With that, they switched up the beat and started to play "Hay" by Crucial Conflict. The crowd went insane. Even other bands were bobbing their heads. It was pandemonium. The rest of the Booker T. band, standing beyond the drumline, all dropped their instruments to the ground and started dancing in place with their hands up in the air.

After about a minute of the band "smokin on hay in the middle of the barn" on the field, the drumline switched up one more time, but this time it was to send a message. They turned, twisted, shouted, free-styled, and then called out the other bands as they broke into a long-forgotten Cameo song. You could hear a collective "Oh shit!" from the stands. Even Southern's band stopped to take notice. And as the drummers played the lyric "Heyyyyyyyyyy, you talking out the side of your neck!" they pointed their sticks at the only band in the competition who may have been a threat, as if to say *We're talking to you*, dropped their sticks, and marched off the field while the rest of our band began playing "Outstanding" by the Gap Band in reference to the BTW Hornet band themselves being outstanding. It was art, it was culture, it was competition, it was dominance. What that band did in the fifteen to twenty minutes they were on the field was like watching Shaquille O'Neal shatter NBA backboards. The feeling was palpable. It was contagious. I'd never seen anything like that before.

The BTW band went on to win the battle and perform the next morning at the Superdome in New Orleans. Sixty thousand people were in the stands, all there to watch the Bayou Classic, but first they would be entertained and then amazed by the Booker T. Washington Hornet band. They stood witness to something special. The stands in the dome were filled from end zone to end zone with HBCU alumni, families, friends, church congregations, and the bands of Southern and Grambling. Every time one of the schools scored, the scoring team's band would play a battle cry out to the opposing team's band. First the horns would go at the other band's horn section. Then the woodwinds. Then the flag girls. Then the drumline and finally the drum majors. There was as much a competition in the stands as there was on the field. This place was holy. It was a mecca. Everything shined. Every sound was triumphant and heavenly. I wasn't competing or performing but I had a feeling I hadn't felt since Mikey was around when I was a kid—included, seen. I felt joy. I knew one thing for sure; when we got back to Tulsa I was going to be in the "often imitated, never duplicated" Hornet band. "You knowwww!"

When Monday came around, I knew what I had to do. I even knew what I was going to say. Because I rehearsed it on the bus ride that morning.

"Coach, I wanna thank you for giving me an opportunity to play on the team, but I wanna take a step away and join the band."

"Bruh, are you serious? You're going to quit a state championship–winning basketball program, with at least eight D1 college players on the team, to play in the BAND?" The voice in my head was in overdrive. *"Nah, mane, you tripping."*

But I wanna do this, I thought, to counter the voice. *I'm doing it. I'ma go talk to Coach Harris after fourth before lunch and I'm out.*

The exasperated voice in my head let out a hiss-like sigh. *Pssssssh, your funeral. You know once you quit you can't come back, right?* I nodded to no one.

I knew the best time to talk to Coach Harris was after fourth period, because he always ate lunch in his office and most likely nobody would be in the field house. I didn't want anyone hearing him yell at me for quitting him for the band. So while sitting befuddled, listening to Mrs. Jackson drone on about planes and vectors in my fourth-period geometry class, I made the decision.

The bell rang so loud it was as if it was antagonizing me, *BZZZZZZZZ time to go put your reputation in the dirt. Ahahahaha.* I quickly dumped my geometry book into my backpack and bolted out the door. "Aye, Dub, you eating lunch here or—" I hit the exit doors so fast Keith couldn't even finish his sentence.

I went straight to the local and statewide–famous Hornet Field House, which sat in the middle of the Booker T. campus. As I yanked on the field house door, the orange-trimmed sidelines and baselines on the court jumped in my face. Trying to not look at the famous floor where so many great high school legends had played, I lifted my eyes up and nine giant state championship banners floated above me, staring down. The banners waved as if a gentle breeze was in the air, but to my mind's eye it looked like they were taunting me, waving *Byeeeeee sucka.* A whisper in my head echoed, *You sure you wanna do this? This is dumb.* Weighed down by self-doubt and unavoidable impending shame, my feet kept shuffling across the court.

When I walked into Coach Harris's office he was sitting at his desk and leaning mid-bite into a sandwich. "Come in, Ellis," he said with a mouthful. "What you need?" I took half a step in, not wanting to close the door behind me. Afraid that if I shut the door he'd jump from behind his desk, rip my head off, and dunk it in the wastebasket at the door.

"Hey, Coach," I muttered.

He looked up from his Subway footlong and squinted. "I can't hear you. Come in." That was exactly the opposite of what I wanted to do. *Damn it,* I thought. I stepped closer to his desk.

I slowly stammered, "Coach, I uhh, I just wanted to . . . to talk to you real quick."

Bite. Chew. Crunch.

"Uh-huh," he hummed. Eyes still on his sandwich. A little mustard on his upper lip. *Just do it,* the voice in my head whispered.

"Coach, I think I'm . . . I should, I mean . . . I'm gonna join the band," I said. Coach Harris stopped mid-chew, dropped his sandwich on the Subway logo–plastered wax paper, and cocked his head to the left as he looked up at me with a raised eyebrow.

"How exactly you gonna do that and be on the team, Ellis?"

I sat in silence for a beat, studying his face. The voice in my head whispered again, *I told you this was stupid.* After what felt like the longest minute I'd ever had in my fifteen years of life, I finally spoke up. "I'm gonna quit the team, Coach."

Coach Harris didn't move a single muscle in his body. It was one of the greatest lessons in stillness I'd ever seen at that point in my life—a lesson I'd use a few years later during a breakup. "You sure that's what you wanna do?" he asked. My mind ran with thoughts: *Yes. Maybe? I think so. I dunno.* I nodded my head yes. Coach Harris took a beat, stood his oddy body up from behind his desk, and reached his giant hand out. "Well, good luck then."

I did about two weeks' worth of band practices before I got tired of being weighed down by the sousaphone. I did love walking out on the field every day after school: I'd flirt, bust a couple jokes, and then once we heard the tap of Mr. Daniels's baton, I'd mosey on over to the brass section to warm up. The band director was tougher than Coach Harris. He could hear you play the wrong note from one hundred yards away. And he would let everybody on the field, and in the stands, know. I was always off because I never practiced on my own. I didn't put in the work. I had been so drawn in by the culture-dripping experience of the Classic, that I hadn't actually considered the amount of work that went into the performance. I was just there because it felt good, and for the social clout. But the reality of it all was that I was running from something— both in band and in basketball. Work ethic over the feeling of being wanted. I gained something invaluable from my Classic experience but I didn't put in the work to be a part of the excellence. And although I liked the band and what it represented, basketball was my love. I needed to find my way back to that same love, passion, and dedication I soaked up from the Battle of the Bands and put it on the court. I just knew it couldn't be with Coach Harris.

THERE'S NO "I" IN TEAM, BUT THERE IS A "ME"

DENVER, CO; TULSA, OK

"So you're saying you're in high school?"

LOVE BASKETBALL. I COULD WATCH IT ALL DAY. DOESN'T MAT-
ter if it's high school, college, WNBA, or NBA. If I had it
my way, while I'm filming, we'd start lunch on set with a game
of five-on-five then break to eat—winner eats first, obviously.
I'm wildly competitive, so after I bust everyone's ankles and
hit the game-winning shot, we'd argue and battle about my
rankings of the greatest players of all time (in no particular
order)—Kobe, Michael, LeBron, Magic, Shaq, KD, the Joker—
before we resumed filming. Every day. We'd do this every day.

BUT BEFORE MY LOVE OF BASKETBALL FORMED, MIKEY AND I TRIED
EVERYTHING. You name it, we tried it.

I tried karate—I didn't like wearing a gi and Mikey didn't
like getting hit. I don't think we even earned a white belt, and
they give those away in the first class. *A nasty, unbathed, toe-
jam-having ten-year-old foot kicking me in the face? Nah, son!*

In third grade I played T-ball on the fields behind the youth center. I lost a pop-fly in the sun once, and by the time Mikey could find the ball it was smashing into my face and dislocating my jaw . . . *Pass.*

In fifth grade I decided to play soccer, but it felt like a lot of work for very little reward. *One or two goals for ninety minutes of running? I'm cool.*

Then there was football. I actually liked football and was okay at it, but I tried it when I was still short and my legs didn't carry me at the speed or length I wanted; I was frustrated and impatient. Plus, you couldn't see my face in a helmet and, well, I'm an actor for a reason.

For a few months I took piano lessons, but you need one at home and the only keyboard I ever had got stolen from our apartment. My dad thought our neighbor did it. And let them know he knew. We didn't see them for weeks after he yelled at them through their door.

I tried playing guitar and Mikey thought I could be the next B.B. King. I took lessons for three weeks, so I'm not sure about that one.

Since most of the places I lived in were hot in climate, swimming was a natural and refreshing choice. I know what you're thinking but I was a great swimmer . . . Mikey couldn't swim. I would drag Mikey to the pool on McClellan Air Force Base every chance I got . . . because I loved having something I was better than him at. Even if it was drying my skin out with the gallons of chlorine they used to try and kill the urine-yellow hue the pool water had.

I did run track for a bit. Mikey didn't like being out in the sun all day and running.

I auditioned to sing in the church choir, but the choir director told me, "Some of God's angels are meant to serve him in other ways."

And finally, before I started playing basketball, I thought about joining the debate team, but that felt like more school.

BY THE TIME I CAME AROUND TO PLAYING BASKETBALL, I HAP-pened to have just gone through a crazy growth spurt. It was as if the hoop gods had perfectly mapped it out. I grew eight inches in about ten or eleven months, becoming the tallest kid in my class. Eight inches. Awkward AF. Between the spring of seventh grade and the start of basketball season in eighth grade I went from shorter than my mom, five-seven, to taller than my dad, six-four. So naturally I thought I was a man.

At thirteen years old and going into eighth grade, Mikey sightings were nonexistent. Everything in my life was starting to change, though. My voice was a little deeper and I had a little taco meat growing on my chest. I hadn't visualized Mikey in a while, but he wasn't "out of sight, out of mind." I could sometimes hear his voice weighing in on important de-cisions. It was self-talk . . . but with Mikey's voice.

My love for basketball came from the first moment I actu-ally competed. From then on, ball was life. And because it was so all-consuming, I learned a lot of important life lessons on the court: listening, reading opponents' body language, and knowing when not to try and muscle my way through something to prove I was right. What being a teammate actu-ally means. These lessons spilled into the streets too, when coming home from practice, going to parties, or kicking it at Tulsa's yearly Juneteenth celebration.

My first year at Byrd Middle School, my now longer, gan-glier limbs got a lot of attention. I had no intention of trying out for the team. But every time one of my friends would try to talk me into it, I'd hear Mikey's voice in my head.

"You gotta do this. Just try it. You're tall. You can be good."

But before I tried out, I had to get ready. I just didn't know how.

"If you watch it, you'll be good." It sounded a lot like Mikey.

Those few weeks before tryouts, I watched every basket-ball game on TV. I stared at my basketball cards—most of which I still have. I carried a basketball around for weeks. I'd walk to the nearest library and read book after book about the game. Lastly, I watched movies about basketball: *Basketball Diaries, Hoosiers, He Got Game,* and *White Men Can't Jump.*

Basketball Diaries taught me how taking heroin will lead to me stealing and prostituting myself until Ernie Hudson comes to save me. *Hoosiers* made me realize I did not want Gene Hackman as a coach! *He Got Game* was full of revela-tions. Who knew Denzel could hoop and Ray Allen could act? And Rosario Dawson . . . teenage me says, *Thank you, Spike. White Men Can't Jump* was the best tutorial on how to talk shit on the court. And also a reminder that some white boys *can* jump. Don't get caught slipping. *Love & Basketball* would be on this list but it came out while I was in high school— I learned something completely different from that movie. Teenage me also says, *Thank you, Gina.*

By the time tryouts came around I had more theoretical knowledge of the game than anyone my age could possibly have. I was gonna kill that tryout. There was one little hiccup I hadn't anticipated. I had zero practical experience. In all my obsessive reading, watching, and basketball-card trading I never actually played a game against other people. Sure, I shot a few free throws in my driveway but free throws don't mean shit in a tryout. Nada. Zero. Zilch. You don't even shoot free throws in a tryout. I have no idea what I was thinking but there I was, walking into the gym for what I had now built up as the biggest day in my life, not knowing what it felt like to actually run up and down the court dribbling the ball while someone in front of me is trying to steal said ball. Honestly, it was a low-down dirty shame.

There were about forty kids in that tryout. A team typically carries twelve. All I could think was twenty-eight souls were going to be crushed that day! Twenty-eight dreams of hitting the game-winning shot were going to be erased. Twenty-eight disappointed looks in parents' eyes as they lied and told their kid, "That's okay! You'll make it next year." Twenty-eight underachievers were going to find out their fate was being a kid in the stands, not on the court. And as I started to descend into a middle school basketball spiral of shame (I'm still that dramatic), we all lined up on the baseline and the coach running the tryout told us there was going to be an A, B, and C team, so we'd all end up on a team. My hoop dreams still lived. *Yessssssss!!!!!!!*

———

DURING MY TIME PLAYING BASKETBALL, THE CONCENTRATION OF real-time lessons on work ethic, teamwork, attitude, and how not to react in life was greater than for any other social activity I'd had to that point. Since I started playing in middle school, there has always been something that happened on the court that could be applied at various times in my life. Even if it wasn't happening directly to me.

Practice for my summer AAU team typically started up toward the end of the school year and began about thirty minutes after school ended. Even though the team wasn't affiliated with the school, we practiced at the youth center that was directly across from campus. Thirty minutes was exactly enough time to holla at the girl you had a crush on before she got on the bus, eat whatever dry snack you snuck out of the cafeteria, and then run across the street and to the locker room to get changed for practice. There wasn't a lot of room for adding other pursuits, but every once in a while someone rolled the dice. And this particular day it was Keith.

We all lined up on the baseline, cracking jokes. "Ah, yo' pants always look like you walked through a flood." "Yo' momma so old, Jesus is yo' real dad." "You stupid. Jesus ain't even—" Until the door at the far end of the gym slammed and Coach walked in. The air shifted, the humidity a little more stifling. Silence.

Coach wasn't very tall, but what he lacked in height he had in intimidation. His eyes sunken in like he worked 365 straight night shifts in an emergency room. Gray hairs creeped into his beard and temples. His round belly protruding in the middle where his waist used to be. He rarely ever smiled, but when he did it made you feel like you won a tournament. Looking down at the court as if it were speaking to him of days of anguish in years past, he barely raised his voice and said, "Five laps."

He may have also just been hungover and unable to yell,

due to a headache. Rumor was Coach hit that bottle like kids drank Gatorade . . . all the time.

We started running circles around the court. Bryan whispered to the group: "Where Keith at?" We all looked around and shrugged. Not sure if Coach had the best hearing in the world or if he read Bryan's mind—both plausible—but by the time most of our shrugged shoulders dropped back into place, he yelled:

"Where's Keith at?!"

Still running, we knew better than to stop; we all looked at each other and a few of us mumbled, "I don't know." That was all that was said. After our five warmup laps we did some stretching, lunges, lateral slides, and a few dribbling drills. And just as we finished up, about twenty minutes into practice, Keith flew into the gym, outta breath.

Keith was short for a guard and built more like a running back. He was one of those guys that there wasn't a girl he hadn't tried to get at. Which was why he was late to practice.

Keith burst through the door looking like a disheveled pile of moving clothes.

"I was helping Mrs. Johnson clean her classroom after her eighth-period kids destroyed it in a paper fight." Laughs came from the ridiculousness of Keith's lie to Coach. His excuse game was weak, but Keith was our starting point guard and, like the rest of us, Coach knew we couldn't win without him on the court. So, without a warmup, Keith jumped into practice. Cold and tight. No time to settle into practice.

As the scrimmaging portion of practice got under way, Coach walked us through a simple play he wanted both teams to run on offense. The point guard (Keith) would bring the ball up the court. Pass it to a wing (me). He would then follow the pass to set a screen for the player he'd passed to (me). The big man down low would post for a few seconds and move if he didn't get the ball. So, with the big man cleared out, the point guard (Keith) and the wing (me) could pick-and-roll.

In most situations the defense will inevitably make a mistake. They could back off the shooter and give him too much space—for a wide-open jumper—or get too close to get over the top of the screen, making it easy for the offensive player to drive to the basket. Or they could get confused on switching or fighting through the screen, creating the easy pick-and-roll motion. And the latter is exactly what happened.

Keith brings the ball up the court, passes to me on the wing; the guy guarding me gets really close to get over the screen. Keith sets the pick. Using Keith's pick, I beat my man going to my left and down the lane, but Keith's man comes to help. Keith rolls to the basket. I, as a natural facilitator, pass it to him. He takes one loooooong step and *CRAAAAAAACK*. He crashes to the floor screaming, rolling back and forth in the most agonizing pain I have ever witnessed.

Everyone on the court froze. My skin tingled and my stomach started to do backflips. Coach yelled for us to help Keith up. A few players closer to him moved to pick him up and Keith screamed more. Tears streamed down his face. My eyes darted between Keith and the bleachers lining the walls. It was too hard to watch. I wanted to help but felt useless at the same time. After about ten to fifteen minutes of Keith laid out on the floor, Coach finally talked him into standing so they could get him to the car and then to the hospital. With Coach on one side and our big man, Ronaldo, on the other, Keith hopped out of the gym and into Coach's car.

The next day, Coach told us to take a seat on the stands before we started practice. He told us Keith had to get surgery, that his season was over, and most importantly that his injury had been preventable. He talked to us about distraction and how even in its most innocent forms, it can take us off course from the things we know we need to be doing to play our best.

Apart from Coach's TED Talk on distraction, one of the things I learned the most from Keith's surgery-causing injury was to prepare (stretch) and warm up (study) as much as, and maybe even more than, I actually work (perform, write, or pitch). Giving myself the space to think through or mimic situations or performances before they actually happen has been huge in my life. There's a moment when it feels like everything around you slows down and you're so locked in and present you can only focus on this thing at hand. Doing it enough becomes second nature. The mind and body just take over and do what you've prepared and practiced. I also use all those visualization exercises, mental warmups, that coaches tell you about. Like "Picture yourself shooting and it going in the basket." I still visualize today.

—

Jameel and Lewis were probably two of the best players on our team. Lewis was the coach's son and had an above-average basketball IQ for his age. He understood the game. He was also mad competitive. He didn't take losing well and always gave maximum effort. Jameel, on the other hand, was a specimen of an athlete. Fast. Strong. Never-ending stamina. If he knew the basic fundamentals of any given sport, he could probably be really good at it. And he knew this. Which meant he didn't work as hard as everyone else, because athletically no one could keep up with him.

Usually in practice these two played on the same team, but sometimes Coach would switch things up if he thought we were getting complacent. Apparently, halfway through one particular practice, Coach saw complacency. Lewis and Jameel went from teammates to guarding each other on opposite teams.

Before I say anything else, I want to state for the record that both of these guys talked way too much trash. For Lewis it was more a tactic to get in your head. For Jameel it was arrogance in knowing that he was better than you and you couldn't guard him.

Talking trash in basketball is an art. Not everyone can do it well, and you have to have a game that can back up the wild statements that come out the side of your neck. When the two match up—gift of game and uncanny ability to decimate someone with your epigrammatic wordplay—it's revered. Think Wesley Snipes in *White Men Can't Jump*. When the two don't match up, which is usually when an average player has an above-average trash talk game and goes too far, it leaves the trash-talker getting exposed on the court. Think Ruben Patterson calling himself "the Kobe Stopper" and the subsequent 40-point games Kobe gave him after.

With Lewis and Jameel guarding each other, my excitement level was like the Michael Jackson meme: eating popcorn at the movies. I wanted a front-row seat!

Lewis knew guarding Jameel was going to be tough for him. He also knew that he needed an edge. So, he started his shit-talking from the jump. Jameel wasn't too fazed by it but with each trip up and down the court, Lewis started to get more specific. It all came to a head with Jameel coming off a screen on the baseline and popping out to the wing, leaving Lewis fighting through the screen. Jameel, wide open, pulls up for a long jumper and Lewis runs toward him with his hands in the air.

"Two for fourteen!"

Doesn't sound like something that should ignite the equivalent of World War III at a basketball practice, but it did.

In our previous game, which we lost by three points, Jameel only made two of the fourteen shots he took. In the locker room after the game, Lewis kept saying that if Jameel would have just passed the ball twice instead of shooting it, we would have won. Statistically, probably unprovable. If you know basketball, sure it's possible, but it's also a leap. The two of them probably would have gone at it and started swinging as soon as Lewis finished his out-of-pocket hot take, but Coach stepped in and told them both to "shut up." He said, "We lost because we didn't make free throws and we had too many turnovers." But as two teenage boys in their feelings who lived in a world that didn't teach boys how to communicate and use their words to express themselves . . . Obviously neither of them heard what Coach had to say.

"Two for fourteen" was a wound that had not healed, and Lewis ripped the scab off without warning. Jameel missed the jumper.

Practice was minutes from being over; Coach called it so we could go over what we learned for the day and what we were going to work on the next day. Jameel mean-mugged Lewis the entire time. Not saying a single word. Eyes narrow and dark, like Mike Tyson in the ring.

After our huddle, we crashed into the crammed locker room. Rusted lockers, much older than us, were lined in multiple rows from the front of the space to the back. There were open showers to the right and bathroom stalls to the left. A few guys headed into the showers; others just changed back into their clothes. Lewis, an avid believer in the after-practice shower, was in his boxers heading to the showers. His locker was on the far end of the row, so he had to cross through the maze of early-teenage hoop zombies and nose-curling after-practice stench to get to the showers on the right side.

About midway through Lewis's journey of the hooping dead was Jameel. Lewis, not thinking anything of it, playfully tagged Jameel on the shoulder.

"Jumper was off, huh?" Now, I'm not sure if that shoulder hit was the dunk that shattered the backboard, or if Jameel had already planned on what he'd do the next time he saw Lewis, but either way, Lewis was about to learn he shouldn't have brought up Jameel's two-for-fourteen performance.

As soon as Lewis's hand lifted off of Jameel's shoulder, Jameel was up and swinging. Lewis screamed. "What the hell, man?!!"

But in that moment, Jameel only knew one way to answer. More punches. Lewis could barely defend himself, slipping on his shower sandals. The entire team yelled for Jameel to stop but he was in a fugue state. Lewis threw his towel at Jameel and grabbed at an open locker door to keep his balance. Jameel used that locker door to slam into Lewis's face, and a tooth flew across the aisle and hit one kid in the face before it rattled to the floor.

About a minute later it was all over. Jameel was hunched over and out of breath and Lewis was on the ground, his hand covering his mouth while blood oozed out of the holes that not one but two teeth used to call home. Jameel grabbed his bag and stormed out without saying a word. A few of us helped Lewis up, and he sat on the bench like he was the inspiration for Paul Wall's hit—"Sittin' sideways, boyz in a daze . . ." He had no idea what happened.

The next day Coach sat with both the boys, individually of course, and asked what happened. When we started practice that day, Coach told us Jameel would no longer be on the team and Lewis wouldn't play in the next two games. The rest of us, lined up on the baseline, got his "sometimes you gotta let shit go" speech that I still live by today:

> *Every day for the rest of your lives you guys are going to do stuff that's not always going to be the best decision or go the way you wanted to go. Hell, sometimes it might be something somebody does to you. And that stuff, if you don't learn to let it go, is going to eat at you. It's going to drive you crazy. It'll make you an asshole. It'll make you second-guess yourself. It'll make you either too bitter or too afraid to push past it and keep getting back up the next day. Sometimes you gotta let shit go. You can be sad, mad, hurt, whatever for a day, but after that, let it go. Just learn from it and move on . . . Five laps. Go.*

Jameel and Lewis's fight—and the losing streak that followed (we lost four of the next six games . . . I let it go)—

taught all of us to stay calm; stay still but not passive. We didn't always need to be the ones to jump in and react. There are unintended consequences that you can't foresee when you're making decisions in a fugue state. To stay out of danger you have to try—when you can, even if only for a split second— to find a moment to weigh all of the options and how possible scenarios could play out. Coach taught us to not react our way through every situation that wasn't in our control.

ON THE COURT, NOT TO BE CONFUSED WITH "IN COURT"—although I did go to court in eighth grade for breaking the city curfew—I learned that you are truly as strong as your weakest link. There are two choices: Nurture that link . . . or replace it.

THE SUMMER BETWEEN EIGHTH AND NINTH GRADE, I WAS THE weakest link. My AAU team, coached by the assistant varsity coach at the high school, went to Denver to play in the national tournament. One of my teammates, and probably our second best player, was a fourteen-year-old Oklahoma version of Woody Harrelson in *White Men Can't Jump*. No lie. Accent and all. And he could not jump! Seriously. But he could shoot and get to the basket. Coincidentally, he was also named Jay—nickname "White Jay." Kids are mad original. Anyway, White Jay doesn't matter in this story because he got injured and wasn't able to play at the end of the tournament. Don't feel bad for him. He went on to play through high school and in college. Had a great career. Feel bad for me.

Because since White Jay was out, I had to guard every big man we played against in the tournament.

And in our final game, versus a team from Yakima, Washington, that big man was a sixteen-year-old, six-foot-eight-inch-tall *man* weighing well over 250 pounds. I was six-foot-three and might have weighed 168 pounds . . . if I was fully clothed and dunked in water. I don't remember the big man's name, but I do remember thinking, *This dude could beat the shit out of Shaq one-on-one!*—no disrespect, Shaq, I was just a kid.

I was tasked with staying in front of the big man so he couldn't easily get the ball. He was a MOUNTAIN. There was no way I could stay in front of him. So our coach yelled and screamed at me the whole game. He couldn't take me out because size-wise I was all the team had and we were down a player. At first I was determined to do a good job, and a few times down the court, I actually thought I was. Then, as the game went on, I got more and more frustrated. No matter what I did, this dude was always in front of me. I never wished Mikey was around so much in my life. He was probably in some imaginary version of a Beverly Hills–meets–Vegas casino, sitting around a betting table in a hazy smoke-filled room, watching me getting manhandled by the Yakima Terror on TV in front of all his imaginary friends.

By the end of the game, we were getting blown out and the Yakima Terror had scored 20-plus points. It wasn't until about halfway through the fourth quarter that I realized I was in fact the weakest link. Coach yelled at me again to get in front of the Terror, and in a moment of frustration, tired and seeing red, without even thinking, I screamed, "Shut the fuck up, Coach!"

As fast as the entire gym snapped their heads to my words,

Coach called a time-out. "Sit at the end. I don't want to see your face," he said, without looking at me. He walked over to the referees and told them we'd be finishing the game with four players because he wouldn't be playing me for the rest of the game. A few minutes after the game started again, Coach sauntered past me.

"If I were you, I'd transfer, because you'll never play at my school." And before that school year started, I in fact transferred.

I HAD MADE A DECISION IN A FUGUE STATE. ONE THAT CAUSED MY team to lose and caused me the embarrassment of having to transfer schools, because I knew I'd messed up. I vowed to myself to never be the weakest link again, and I have been perfect ever since. The End.

—

MY SENIOR YEAR IN HIGH SCHOOL I WAS THE STARTING POWER forward on my team. I'd had no idea what life was going to be like when I transferred to the school years prior, and even though the dynamics in school were problematic, on the court I was having a great time. I played well and actually really loved most of my teammates. My hair was dyed blond as an homage to Dennis Rodman, because I was a great rebounder. I was already being scouted for college, which was the reason I dedicated myself to ball in the first place—and yes, I'm using this as an opportunity to remind you I played college basketball. I was okay at best but I still played, damn it!

My mom had graduated from college and entered a management training program at her job as a bank executive and my dad, after serving in the Air Force for ten years, was settled in his career as a mechanic for American Airlines. They were doing all right, especially for two Black teenage parents who made it unscathed through Reaganomics and the crack epidemic. They had just bought their first house and, for the first time, we were settled . . . at least for a few years.

Soon after, my parents bought the only luxury car anyone in my family had ever owned. It was a 1996 Lexus LS 400. White exterior with cream seats. It had a premium six-disc CD changer and a car phone. It was smooth. Some would even say "phat." You walked taller when you got out of that car. It was an automatic ego-booster. I dubbed it "Lex Luthor" because the front grill had a grin like a villain's smile. Mikey would have LOVED Lex Luthor. It would have been everything he lived for, to ride around in Lex.

In Tulsa there were only a few types of people who drove a Lex Luthor: executives, doctors, and dope boys. I was none of the above, but it didn't stop me from begging, pleading, and guilting my parents in every way possible into letting me drive Lex. And please believe I used the fact that they'd yanked me out of my predominantly Black school and dropped me in a private school, where I was one of four Black kids, as a weapon against them. And by my senior year, it worked. But driving Lex Luthor came with a lot of rules.

I was told to drive under the speed limit but not too slow. *But Lex Luthor and his V8 engine wouldn't like that. He was an animal ready to attack.*

There were no extracurricular activities allowed. I had to drive straight to school and back. No stops. *Even though the whole purpose of driving the car was to BE SEEN IN THE CAR!* My dad was the epitome of "Homey don't play that."

"Don't have people in the car." My brain did the #black-math (google it). *"People" is plural. So, I could have at least one person in the car.*

When it came to traffic lights the rule was, if a light turns yellow just stop. *But I could also just use this engine to get through it, right?*

My mom, the strict academic, made it very clear: "If your grades slip, no car." Ha. She ain't know this school was way easier than my public school.

The last three rules were:

"If you're late to school, no car." I woke up thirty minutes earlier from then on.

"If you're late coming home from school, no car." That wasn't going to be a problem. I'd just run out of basketball practice in my practice gear to get home on time. No shower.

And the final thing my dad said—which made me realize my parents were telling me all of this through a different lens—"If a cop pulls you over, turn your music off, roll your windows down, and put your hands on the steering wheel. Don't make any sudden movements, and when you do make any moves, make sure you announce them to the officer. Say 'Yes, sir' and 'No, sir.' Don't make too much eye contact, so you don't seem like you're challenging them, but make enough eye contact so they don't think you're up to something."

This was "the Talk." We'll unpack that later, but for now: Picture me rollin'!! (RIP 2PAC.)

For the first few months, Lex Luthor and I were gliding

through the streets of South Tulsa like we owned all the kryptonite in the world. Everyone at school—teachers, staff, and students—would stare open-mouthed at me as I'd pull in and out of the parking lot every day. My Nakamichi sound system banging Jay-Z's "Imaginary Player," as a subconscious homage to Mikey. I pushed the limits of what the speakers could handle. I was a king sitting on my luxury Japanese imported throne. With keys in my hand, I had dreams of running my city like a Prince runs Houston.

It didn't take some horrific accident or racing experience gone wrong for me to understand why my parents gave me all of those rules. It was the moments I wasn't doing anything "wrong" when I learned the most about why they were so anxious every time I walked out of the door.

The first time I got pulled over, I panicked. Like any well-adjusted teenager should do. I didn't panic because I was afraid of what the cop would do, but because I was scared my parents were going to try and break me and Lex up. I wasn't naive, but this was my first time by myself with a cop. It's different.

Driving down Sheridan Road just before I made the turn down my street, I heard the unmistakable ear-piercing screech of a police siren. I looked in front of me first to see if I could spot a cop ahead. Nope. I cranked my head to the left and looked in the side-view mirror and saw the police car, in my lane and closing in behind me. My foot slid off the accelerator and I moved my eyes to the rearview mirror. He was already directly behind me. His red and blue strobes bouncing off the mirror into my eyes. I pulled into a gas station that a few years earlier had served as my bus stop to my previous school,

Booker T. My heartbeat rose, my armpits began gushing sweat, and my knees got weak. As if it were a mantra, I heard my dad's voice:

Turn your music off, roll your windows down, and put your hands on the steering wheel. Don't make any sudden movements, and when you do make any moves, make sure you announce them to the officer. Say "Yes, sir" and "No, sir." Don't make too much eye contact, so you don't seem like you're challenging them, but make enough eye contact so they don't think you're up to something.

And so, I did. As the officer slowly approached with his cocky swagger, his chest puffed out and face scrunched up like he just drank a bitter beer, I racked my brain for what I could have done wrong. What traffic rule did I break?

The officer stood with his hands on his belt. Lowered his sunglasses. Stared at me for a beat. The stench of days-old coffee gone stale on his breath.

"This car yours?" he said.

"Yessir." His left eyebrow raised.

"You an athlete?"

"Yessir."

"Who do you play for?"

"Magnet Charter," I said. The officer sighed.

"So you're saying you're in high school?"

"Yes."

"License and registration, and step out of the vehicle and stand at the front of the car with your hands on the hood."

What was a normal day of me doing what my parents asked, hurrying home from basketball practice, turned into me standing—in the bone-chilling cold of winter, wearing shorts and sweat-soaked T-shirt—with my hands on the hood of my car for forty-five minutes while every set of eyes driving through South Tulsa that frigid afternoon gawked.

The officer asked me the same few questions on repeat. He'd then walk back to his car and sit for a few minutes with all my answers—this happened five times. It took the cop forty-five minutes to believe my license, my registration, and my story were real. No ticket. No warning. No reason for pulling me over. I was embarrassed. I was pissed. I was crushed. I couldn't understand *Why me?* Or *What have I done wrong?* I knew, but in the moment too many thoughts flooded my mind to accept the reality.

After the officer let me go, I sat in my car for another ten minutes. I needed to warm up from being outside in the cold, and I needed to spiral through the rush of confused and conflicting emotions I was feeling. I went home that day and never told my parents about it.

I got pulled over eight more times that year. Nine times total. I never got a citation or a ticket. And I never told my parents about any of the stops. Unfortunately, I got used to something no one should get used to: the pattern of looks and questions and having to prove I was in a car that I didn't steal.

Is this your car? Are you an athlete? What team you play for? Are you currently on any drugs or narcotics? Do you have a weapon in the car? Do you have any drugs or narcotics in the car? Does the owner of this car know you are driving it? Where did you get this car?

Each time, my soul got crushed a little more. Not able to process all of the layers I was facing: prejudice, racism, bias, and adultification. These cops saw and treated me as if I were an adult. My stories and experiences were different than the ones my classmates at my private school were having in the rare instances they were pulled over.

These officers were essentially doing a version of stop-and-frisk every time they saw me driving Lex Luthor. They were stopping me because they had a "feeling "or a "hunch" that as a Black kid, in this part of town, I had to be driving a stolen vehicle.

At the time I first got the keys—and rules—for Lex Luthor, I thought my parents were just being overprotective because their only son was driving out into the world and flossing with a V8 engine, but as I sat there time after time with a flashlight shining in my face and being asked to step out of the car, I began to understand that they were nervous parents who were trying to protect me from the cruel realities of driving while; teaching me how to live through a "routine stop" and not make the nightly news.

All my friends' parents had given them the Talk. It has been an ugly rite of passage that has been passed from Black parents to their children since the day the automobile became common in Black households. I dread the day that I have to give the Talk.

BASKETBALL, AND ALL OF THE THINGS IT BROUGHT INTO MY LIFE, gave me the perfect opportunity to learn how to navigate life post-Mikey in this world where I was no longer seen as a kid. It protected me in a lot of ways. It kept me out of trouble. It gave me something to look forward to and it created long-lasting friendships, memories, and opportunities in my life.

After that first time I made the team in middle school, Mikey was no longer a voice in my head. All I had was my day-to-day experiences and my subconscious to guide me. With basketball I learned how to be a teammate. What it means to be accountable and hold others accountable. I learned that it's always about the next play. If you dwell on the last one then you're not present. I learned preparation, focus, and visualization. And I learned that making a decision in an agitated state could have unforeseen and unintended lifelong consequences. In a lot of ways many of my coaches (though not all of them) were a form of role model as well.

AMONGST COMPANY

TULSA, OK

"One kid asked me if I wore underwear because
he saw a documentary where the men in some
remote African tribe went commando . . ."

I N THE LATE '90S, AFTER MOVING TO A CITY THAT REGULARLY
had KKK rallies on the city hall steps, I was in one of the
deadliest and longest ongoing conflicts known to human-
kind, the four-year voyage through high school, and I was
doing it all without my best friend, Mikey, by my side. In the
past he had been there to guide me through the land mines
and surprise ambushes of preteen and adolescent life. He
helped me pick out my Girbaud jeans and my FUBU tops
years before. He told me if my haircut was "straight trash"
and, after complaining about my nonexistent waves, he told
me to shave it all off and start over if I wanted to get folks
seasick with my 360-degree waves (I didn't figure this out
until college, and I had 'em woozie).

The stakes were constantly rising. Mikey had left years
ago because somewhere along the way I didn't have the luxury of time, or innocence, or being without responsibility
and consequences. All of a sudden I was unable to give my-

self enough space and quiet to reflect, to play, to imagine, to create, because I was constantly being tested and challenged and was fighting in a different way. I stopped being able to conjure Mikey, or maybe I was too overwhelmed to even think of him.

In the middle of my sophomore year, two things happened that led to my parents making me transfer schools. First, my grades had dramatically fallen because I was "having too much fun!" and my mom wasn't about it. And second, I wasn't going to make the varsity basketball team at my previous school on account of me quitting the team. And I had to make the team. That's how I was going to get a college scholarship. That's how I'd make it to the NBA. And that's how I'd cash that $100 million check from the Seattle Supersonics that was hanging behind an MLK magnet on our refrigerator.

That check represented both my love for basketball and Kevin Garnett getting the first $100 million contract in NBA history. It was the first future-me goal I had ever really set.

I had a plan that I had to stick to. As for my parents, I'm sure they realized how playing basketball kept me motivated but more importantly kept me out of trouble. So that January, in the middle of the school year, I transferred from Booker T. Washington High School to Magnet Charter Academy.

BOOKER T. WAS A PREDOMINANTLY BLACK SCHOOL ON THE NORTH side of town where for 99.9 percent of the student body, I was "different." I talked "different" because I pronounced my *r*'s in words like *hair* or *here*. I was "different" because I read books—thanks, Mom—and because I cared about getting good grades so I could go to college. Even my looks weren't up to par. I didn't sag my pants—therefore, yet again, I was "different"—and after a change in chairs at the shop my haircuts were always a little off, the handiwork of "Tyrone da Barber."

Tyrone added "da Barber" to his name after Erykah Badu's megahit "Call Tyrone" came out and ruined every dude named Tyrone's life.

As much as I got tired of people copying my homework, I also enjoyed being "different." I had grown to like it; I was doing my thing. I wore it with pride.

But all of that "different" talk at Booker T. was superseded by a new set of high school dynamics and group norms in the foreign world of Magnet.

At Magnet, just like at Booker T. my freshman year, I was thrown into a new environment, with more factors and pressures, and as a fifteen-year-old boy I constantly had the overwhelming feeling—and reality—of surviving as "one of the only." But this time for a different reason.

After a year and a half at Booker T., I ended up across town where I was one of four Black kids in a K–12 private school that before my arrival had a collective median melanin measurement of –52. This school wasn't terribly hard to get into—it accepted everyone as long as you could afford the tuition or they deemed you worthy of a scholarship (I got a partial scholarship).

On my first day as a transfer from Booker T. Washington, I was given the responsibility to be the senior authority on all things Black. Me, the kid who was one of the few "different" kids at the Black school, was now the go-to for all things Black and urban. Please believe, I had a lot of fun making shit up.

A few years ago, when I watched Cersei, from *Game of Thrones*, walk through the streets butt-naked while the entire village violently chanted "shame, shame, shame," it reminded me of walking through the halls of MCA for the first time. But instead of "shame" chants, kids', counselors', and teachers' eyes were filled with confusion, rage, excitement, wonder, and hate.

It was January, which for most of the Midwest meant it was cold and gray. The halls of the school were wide—they had the luxury of space at this school, nothing was crammed. The walls were made of dark red brick that looked like years of caked-up dried blood. Pictures of every senior class in the school's history lined the hall. Little kids, five or six years old, held hands and sang "Yes, Jesus loves me" as they followed their fresh-out-of-college teacher to the elementary classrooms.

About forty feet down the hall, just past the headmaster's office—for the next two years, every time I heard the word *headmaster* I would have an out-of-body experience where I became Toby from *Roots*—I was broken out of my environment-induced shock by a thick Southern drawl.

"Dood, we ca' use you on'a football team. I bet you sup'a fast," said Roy. Roy was a snaggletoothed, steak-and-potato-eating Neanderthal of a junior, who happened to be the captain of the football team.

Roy had spent the majority of his life watching Black athletes dominate the sport he loved. So he was excited at what my arrival to the school meant for his dreams of winning a championship. Roy didn't know my name, yet he had the intuition of a storefront psychic to bet that I was "super fast."

He was right, by the way, I was fast. Long legs and all.

"Yeah, I'm fast but I don't play football," I said as I continued to walk. Roy's face soured.

"You're Black. You gotta be good at football." As a fifteen-year-old in the '90s, I only knew to take Roy's comment on my supposed predisposed "Black" football ability as a compliment. On one hand, sure, it was odd to me that Roy insisted I was the second coming of Jerry Rice, but on the other hand, someone thought I was good at something and, more specifically, thought I could save the sluggish, below-average, rarely-having-had-a-winning-season football team that he loved. I hadn't played football since Pop Warner, so I'm sure I was trash, but for a split second I thought maybe Roy was right; the veiled guise of Roy's urbanity-deficient approval made me think maybe he was right.

Throughout the course of that first week, every coach in the school tried to recruit me to come play on their team. The football coach told me I'd only have to practice one day a week to run plays—he had never even seen me play football. The track coach told me he would drop me off at home after school if I wanted to run—running for him felt too close to running from him. Another coach, who also taught at the school, told me to sign up for his class 'cause he'd "take it easy" on me if I was one of his "boys."

Where I'm from, when a grown man says "boys" it means one of two things—I wasn't sure if he was a pedophile or a racist; he was probably neither, but I knew either way I didn't want to be one of his "boys" and find out.

I was expected to be the best football player, baseball player, and track athlete in the entire school. I dodged all of it and instead found my way to the basketball coach.

On the court I was good. Untouchable. Kids, parents, and

teachers cheered my name from the very second I stepped on the court until after the game ended, when I came out of the locker room dressed in street clothes. During the school week, however, it was a different vibe. Sure, I got a few high fives and "right on's" from a few people, but most of the school day I was in a bubble. Only talking to my teammates and a few others.

It took a few months for me to find my footing, or the illusion of footing, but I eventually found myself somewhat settled in this alien land. I had built walls and masks to protect myself from the constant gaze of my classmates and teachers, whose eyes lasered and burned through me like sunlight through a magnifying glass melting a G.I. Joe. Their constant line of questions on hip-hop, fashion, haircuts, sports, and all things cultural became easier to deal with. But no matter how high I built those walls or how much I fortified them, something always got through. Doesn't matter what you tell yourself; after a thousand paper cuts, you're going to bleed.

And after you bleed and those walls and masks have served their purpose, you have to learn how to grow from those moments and pivot. Fortunately for the performer in me, I get to do this every day at work, but back then I was stumbling through it.

The first of the deep cuts was thanks to Mr. Theater Teacher, the theater teacher at Magnet. He had spent over a decade teaching at the high school and putting on the same play, *Oklahoma!*, over and over again. I wanted to participate in the arts in some way, so I decided I should try my luck at acting in this new school. Even before I'd found my sousaphone calling back at Booker T., Mikey and I used to play all the time in a way that I later came to realize was me performing, acting, and role-playing. I was creating characters and improvising long before I knew what any of it actually meant.

Mr. Theater Teacher was set to hold his uninspired try-outs for that semester's production of *Oklahoma!* about six weeks after school started. When I found out, I expressed my interest to him during lunch.

"Hey, Mr. Theater Teacher, I wanna sign up for auditions," I said, hovering over him at his table.

Mr. Theater Teacher looked up through his LensCrafters frames while his fork scraped across his plate.

"What character?" he grumbled.

"I was thinking Will."

There was a beat of silence between us that grew into tension as thick as the meatloaf on his plate. He dropped his fork, pushed his lunch tray away, and looked up at me from his seated position.

"I don't think you're the Will type." No explanation. No plan B. He turned back to his food, dismissing me.

I walked away, unsure how to process his reaction. Ultimately I let it go and decided to focus on the upcoming basketball season. But little did I know there was another cut coming my way—one that would involve Mr. Theater Teacher.

Liam was a doughy, below-average, spray-tanned lump of a human, who—even though he lived in the middle of a metropolitan city with 400,000 people—wore worn-in cowboy boots to school every day like he just got done herding his family's cattle that morning. His family lived in a normal, quiet Tulsa suburb. Not a ranch.

Liam's girlfriend, LeAnn, came from a pretty wealthy family. Her dad owned a medium-sized oil company that afforded them vacation homes, private planes, lake houses, and a brand-new Mercedes for LeAnn. She was a huge come-up for Liam. She was also good friends with my best friend.

I never spent much time around Liam. We didn't have any classes together, and none of our after-school activities crossed either. The little I knew about him I had either observed in the "hallway" as we moved from class to class, or had heard secondhand from other kids. Of all the things people said about him, the overwhelmingly consistent message was that he was racist.

Malachi, one of the three other Black kids at Magnet and one of my closest friends, whom I met when we first moved to Tulsa, was a class favorite. Everyone loved him. Malachi had been at Magnet for a few years, and although he had come from a much more diverse middle school, he had found his way to survive and navigate Magnet. No shade, but with his charisma it was clear he was going to take Bill Bellamy's job on MTV *Beach House* one day. He had a way of making the kids in school feel comfortable, at ease with him—usually through jokes. One of those students was LeAnn.

Malachi and LeAnn sat next to each other in their third-period Social Studies class. A class that made even the most fastidious of students fall into the dark abyss of boredom. One day, while bored in class, Malachi drew his name in graffiti letters on LeAnn's arm. *Malachi*.

Malachi for sure knew that LeAnn and Liam were dating. When Liam leveled up and LeAnn decided to slum it, it was the talk of the school for weeks. But Malachi was bored, a boy, and didn't think anything of it.

The main building of Magnet was a uniquely built structure for a school. For starters, there weren't any hallways. The

main building at Magnet was a rotunda. All of the classrooms
were on the outside of the circle, and in the middle sat an
open-air library with shortened waist-level shelves. Unlike a
typical hallway, where you couldn't necessarily see everything
happening at the other end, the "hall" at Magnet allowed for
everyone to easily look across the rotunda and see whatever
was happening on the other side.

After the bell rang at the end of third period, everyone
spilled into the rotunda. Liam met up with LeAnn to walk her
to her next class. From the accounts that I heard, he saw
LeAnn from across the rotunda and a big goofy smile spread
across his face as he moved toward her. She hummed an
Alanis Morissette song, her favorite, as Liam approached her.
Upon his approach he looked down to grab her hand and his
smile slowly turned into a rage scowl. Liam pulled LeAnn's
arm closer to his face to inspect her new forearm tattoo.

"What is that?" Liam's eyes turned red, horns grew from
his head, and smoke started to fly out of his nose as he pulled
his metaphorical white hood out of his back pocket, tossed it
over his head, and yelled.

"You let that nigger draw on you?"

I was on the other side of the rotunda, and the hairs on
the back of my neck stood up at hearing someone use the
N-word. I stopped dead in my tracks and turned my attention
across the rotunda. No one else even so much as stutter-
stepped. They all kept moving, which said to me this was way
too normal in this school. To get around the rotunda we were
instructed by the librarian that we needed to walk around the
library's perimeter. No one was allowed to take a shortcut
through her outdated and culturally bankrupt curation of
books, or else she'd write you up. Normally, I followed her

rule. But this day was different. I didn't care about getting written up.

I crossed through the library, and one of the first people I could see while in my fugue state was Tabitha, who was the lone woman and fourth member of the Black card–carrying students of Magnet. Pissed and hurt, tears poured down her face after hearing Liam so effortlessly and fearlessly call Malachi a nigger. I approached Liam as he still berated LeAnn with questions about why she'd let Malachi draw on her arm.

"What did you just say?" I asked Liam. He turned to me with an indignant smug grimace.

"What?" he said.

I know Liam heard what I said but I wanted to give him the benefit of the doubt. I wanted Liam to say he fucked up. I wanted him to apologize and beg me not to whoop his ass. I wanted him to realize that that word was hateful, not to be played with, and that he should never, ever say it again. So, I asked again with fire rushing through my body.

"What did you just say?"

Liam glanced at LeAnn, then back at me. "I said, you let that nig—"

Unlike LeAnn's favorite artist, Alanis Morissette, I did not have one hand in my pocket and the other one giving a peace sign. Instead I reached back to Rosa Parks sitting on a bus, Malcolm X saying "By any means necessary," and Marcus Garvey defiantly standing tall, with "Mamma Said Knock You Out" scoring the moment, and punched Liam square in the nose.

He screamed "OWWWWWWW" as his hands shot up to his face. Blood sprayed from his nose.

"What the fuck, man?" he cried. I'm not sure if he really

didn't understand why he just got punched or if he was shocked someone hit him for doing so, but I didn't care.

Just to be clear, up until this point in my academic career, I had never been the aggressor. Except for that one time that led to me temporarily joining a gang in middle school. I'd defended myself, sure, but I wasn't swinging on folks regularly. In fact, in most cases I tried to defuse tension with a joke or something I thought would lighten the mood and distract people, but this moment was different.

Never having been in this situation before, I had no idea what to say to Liam's dumbass question. I wished Mikey were there to whisper something slick in my ear. But nothing came. So after a long beat, with everyone in the rotunda watching, I took a step closer to Liam and said the first thing that ran through my mind.

"You ain't shit. You're just like your daddy. You don't do shit, and you never gonna amount to shit." Yes, the only thing I could think of in my triumphant awe-inspiring moment of racial justice was a line of dialogue from Mrs. Baker in *Boyz N the Hood*.

Before Liam could respond, a few students stepped in to split us up. Teachers were starting to part the sea of lookyloos and make their way to the scene. Ms. VanNueman, Coach Detono, and last but not least Mr. Theater Teacher.

Mr. Theater Teacher pushed his way through the students and arrived just as I finished my *Boyz N the Hood*–inspired retort to the slur-throwing lump of dough standing in front of me. As the blood trickled down Liam's nose, Mr. Theater Teacher demanded to know what was going on.

"What's happening here?" he asked. Liam lifted his hand from his nose so the teachers could get a better look.

"He hit me outta nowhere. I didn't do anything."

"Did you hit him?" Mr. Theater Teacher said.

"Yep. He called Malachi a nigger and I'd do it again if he said it again." With the exception of Eric back on that bus in middle school, I had never physically started a fight to prove my point, but I'd endured the last paper cut I could stand. I was going to make sure everyone at Magnet knew that I stood in opposition to their willingness, passiveness, and complicity to use or let other kids use the N-word. It was like something possessed my body and wanted everyone in that rotunda to know: *Play if you want, but know I busting heads if y'all out recklessly tossing the N-word around.*

Mr. Theater Teacher's eyes blinked rapid-fire for ten seconds after I repeated what Liam had said. It was like watching the pinwheel on a Mac computer spin. He looked at me and yelled, "Office!" Sending me, and only me, to the headmaster's office. Mr. Theater Teacher made an allowance for racism.

I turned and walked to the office with my head held high, flashing a smile just so everyone could see how much I enjoyed what I had just done. My expression screaming, *If you got something to say, come see me.* I ended up in my counselor Mrs. Bailey's office for an hour, talking through my anger and frustration. As much as a Black kid in a predominantly white and upper-class private school could, I trusted her. She was by far the most tolerant, sympathetic, and nonracist person in that school. She calmed me down and tried to put together an action plan for me to follow in case something like that happened again. While I probably should have gotten suspended for the actual punch, I ended up getting detention for two days. I think our headmaster didn't want to have to deal with punishing Liam for his use of the N-word, and therefore he gave me a "light" punishment. A difference in treatment that occurred regularly at that school.

Being a fighter was a new mask that I put on that day. It was a persona to help protect not only me but also Malachi, Tabitha, and Mark from bigoted racist behavior. Now don't get me wrong. It wasn't eradicated. It was still Oklahoma. Like when one of my teammates yelled, "Get these niggers off me" to a referee during a game. No technical. No talking-to. Instead, after I brought it up in the locker room at half-time, our assistant coach said, "Don't let dissension amongst the ranks distract us from our goal."

And each time any of the kids slipped and said the N-word, they apologized and begged me not to punch them, which I hated not because I felt bad that they were afraid but because I couldn't understand how they could say something so incredibly hurtful one minute and then be red-faced, nearly in tears, the second they knew they were afraid to be in pain. They didn't care enough to *not* say it. My hurt gave way to anger and frustration.

As angry, tormented, and devastated as I was, I understand now that my classmates and teammates had been indoctrinated since birth. Racism is learned. And since the day these children begin to process the world around them, they were led to believe that they were superior, and that racial epithets were not only okay to use, but even well deserved. I'm sure Liam learned it from his parents, and many of the kids I went to school with came from similar homes. Homes where slurs and daily slights were so ingrained in their day-to-day lives that they never questioned them or had the awareness, curiosity, or education to know that they were wrong.

The kids carried the big and the small with them to school. In no way am I condoning or explaining away their behavior; it was ignorant, hurtful, demeaning, and beyond frustrating. But I am acknowledging where the seeds of discrimination and racism start—at home—and Liam was the cut that opened my eyes to it.

LIAM'S BEHAVIOR UNLOCKED A NEW MASK FOR ME. ONE THAT Mikey had once told me back in the day would instantly shut down anyone trying to annoy or intimidate me: Imitate Ice Cube. So, out of nowhere, in the middle of class, on the playground, or in a restroom, I'd start rapping Ice Cube's most infamous diss track, "No Vaseline." If you know this song, you know how it wonderfully uses colorful and expressive language to aggressively disrespect and call out the rappers Cube had beef with at the time, in the early '90s. If you don't know this song, listen to it, but just know there is no coming back.

Years later and a few months after I transferred to Magnet, I remembered Mikey's trick, which helped to keep daily slights and micro-aggressions at bay. Cue rap lyrics.

ONE OF THE FEW CLASSES MALACHI AND I HAD TOGETHER WAS Mrs. Bethea's science class. Being in that class together gave us one of the rare times when Malachi and I could authentically be ourselves in school. Mrs. Bethea loved experiments. We did something new every week, and on the day after an experiment, class was reserved for writing reports that supported our findings.

Since Malachi and I always partnered up for our experiments, we'd sit next to each other on report day. Which meant very little writing and a whole lot of clowning. Whenever Mrs. Bethea would hear us talking, she'd turn from her desk and reprimand us by making us stand up in front of the class and tell everyone what was so important that we had to interrupt everyone else's time.

Malachi and I had become so in tune with Mrs. Bethea's body language that we were able to predict the exact moment she was going to turn and look out to the class. To save ourselves from punishment, Malachi came up with "Busy Face."

Busy Face was Malachi's way of making teachers think he was doing his classwork when they turned to see who was disrupting class. Seconds before Mrs. Bethea looked in our direction, Malachi would rest his forehead in his left hand between his pointer finger and his thumb, tap his pencil against his lips, and go back and forth from squinting at his paper to looking up at the smoker's-teeth-yellow/water-stained/drop-tile ceiling as if he were waiting for genius to strike. I saw it work one time and I immediately improvised my own. A few students never caught on and couldn't understand how we'd get away with it.

Robby Clark was one of a few class clowns at Magnet. By the school's awe-inspiring low standards, he was also a heartthrob. All the girls liked him. To the guys in the school he was a try-hard who was always trying too hard for a joke. Which was true. Robby always tried to get a big laugh from his classmates. And like a true performer, he was addicted to the high that comes with the immediate feedback you get from a live performance. So he would double down to get another hit, and another and another. He'd go until a deranged Joker-like smile would spread across his face. I didn't mind Robby's jokes. He didn't annoy me as much as he annoyed the rest of the class, but he also never directed any jokes at me. That is, until he couldn't wrap his head around how he kept getting in trouble in Mrs. Bethea's class, and Malachi and I didn't.

One report day, Robby wanted to get the attention of this cute new girl in class named Trier. Robby tried to get Fitch, who sat one seat in front of Robby, to tap the person in front of him to get to Trier, who was two rows ahead of Robby. Fitch was the school hothead, who didn't take shit from anybody. Fitch would strike without warning and everyone knew it. So when Robby tapped him and Fitch said "No," Robby knew that if he pushed again he'd get knocked back to his first-period classroom. So he had to go another route to get Trier's attention.

"Trier . . . TRIER . . . TRIERRRRRR!" Robby crescendoed across the quiet room. Trier finally turned, but so did the rest of the class, and so did Mrs. Bethea. Mrs. Bethea looked over her glasses at Robby.

"Mr. Clark, do you have a scientific breakthrough you'd like to share with the class?" Robby shook his head no. "Well then I guess after-school detention can help you better understand that it's not okay to yell people's names in the middle of class."

Robby's sun-washed blond eyebrows nearly touched, he frowned so hard. "What? No, that's not fair. What about Jay and Malachi? They're back there rapping and you didn't give them detention." Malachi and I made the Busy Face. Mrs. Bethea looked at Robby.

"Two days' detention . . ."

Robby was drowning, grasping at straws. "What? Is it because they're Black?"

There was a collective chuckle that rumbled from one side of the room to the other. Malachi and I went from Busy Face to *Wait! What?* face. But that was it. Robby had gotten his first "joke" of the day in, and now he had to chase the high. His head slightly tilted back, his pupils dilated, and a slightly open-mouthed smile spread across his face. He was in euphoria. So he doubled down. "They're so Black, she can't see them unless they smile . . ."

Don't get me wrong, in the HBCU feeder halls of Booker T., a "You so Black . . ." joke was a multiple-times-a-day, every-day-of-the-week thing. We capped on each other nonstop, and one's darkness or lightness was sadly always fair game—you know, inherited colorism, inherited racialist supremacy. But coming from a blond-haired, light-eyed, boat shoe and khaki–wearing kid—nah, homey! That wasn't going to fly. Ripped from one of the few authentically myself moments I got being in that school, I slipped another of my metaphorical masks on.

Oh hell no! the voice in my head said. *He gon' interrupt our rhyme session with this bullshit? Hit him with it.* Out of nowhere, with the class still cackling at Robby's joke, sitting back in my seat, legs cocked open, I start rapping my own version of the most aggressive song I knew at the time:

First off, fuck your bitch and the shit you claim,
Jay E when I ride come equipped with game,
You claim to be a player but I fucked her twice,
We bust on funny boys, Robby's fucked for life

Mrs. Bethea's eyes went wider than her Coke-bottle glasses. The class went silent. Robby looked like he peed himself.

"Mr. Ellis, I'm not sure what you did at your previous school but we do not use that language at Magnet Charter. Take your things and go see Mrs. Bailey." I felt a few eyes on me as I stuffed my books into my backpack. But I knew Robby wasn't looking, and I knew he would never joke with me again.

In a school that was run like Willy Wonka's Chocolate Factory full of the unaware privileged students of *Clueless,* our counselor, Mrs. Bailey, was by far the coolest adult at Magnet. She didn't judge, and unlike a lot of the other staff in the school, she didn't make you feel like a lost cause who could never be saved. Instead, she left space for you to talk through your feelings.

"Mrs. Bailey, I'm out here trying to survive in these hard-ass privileged private school streets as one of four Black kids in a school of four hundred people. It's rough out there. Do you know what happens in those hallways?! One kid asked me if I wore underwear because he saw a documentary where the men in some remote African tribe went commando all the time—I'm not African, so I don't know, but that sounds like some pretty dumb shit to me!"

After I talked through my feelings with Mrs. Bailey, the headmaster gave me three days of in-house suspension. Robby got one day of after-school detention. This was the consistent and constant heavy-handed judgment that came with being "one of" in a space where you weren't welcome. Robby could throw out a joke that was blatantly racist and

Liam could scream the N-word in front of the entire school and all they got was detention, while I was sent into a sterile room alone for three days.

DURING MY TIME AT MAGNET, I'M NOT SURE I EVER REALIZED that I was slipping these masks on and off. Or that Malachi, Tabitha, and Mike were as well. The only thing I recognized was the jarring feeling of needing to protect myself, which was often provoked by an ignorant comment from a classmate, teammate, teacher, or coach. It would happen when I was at my most unguarded: during a flow state on the basketball court with Matt, trying to beat the bell as I walked between classes with Liam, or acting out Busy Face as I wrote raps with Malachi, with Robby. The masks felt like characters or personas that I'd put on any time I felt in danger, frustrated, and even hurt. I could navigate my new environment best when I wore one of these masks. I could keep myself sane and protected.

Luckily, in a lot of ways, I never wore the "fit in" mask at that school. I think the lack of attachment that comes with moving so much, and having my deeper friendships with my boys outside of Magnet, I never really cared to fit in. Outside of being on the court, which wasn't racial-slur safe, my boys were the only ones I felt safe around, like in my friendship with Mikey. I learned a lot in those two years. Not just in the classroom but in life. I learned my dad's real-life twin was Darius Rucker because all the kids called him "Hootie" every time he came to school. I learned new phrases like "Schwing!" because of my teammates' fervent love for *Wayne's World*. I learned how beautiful of a metaphor for love "Crash into me" was thanks to Dave Matthews. And, because of DMB, I got my first introduction to Jimmy Hendrix from their cover of "All Along the Watchtower," which led to me becoming a massive Hendrix fan. And while at school I wore the masks more and more, outside of school I learned how liberating it was to take them off.

THE SHOW MUST GO ON

LOS ANGELES, CA

"You'll be good. You got this."

I NEVER HAD CLOSURE AFTER MIKEY LEFT. I NEVER SAID GOOD-
bye to him, nor did I say goodbye to most of my childhood friends. We moved so much, I rarely had the opportunity
for closure. Not that I'd want it. I hate goodbyes. I run from
them. Moving around made me resistant to forming attachments; that way, when I'd inevitably move again, I wouldn't
be rocked because I had to say goodbye to people I cared
about but knew I would never see again. Instead, it was on to
the next. But attachments, healthy ones at least, can be good
for us, right? Maybe that's why all these years later I had to
write these stories, I had to write through and about Mikey,
about my childhood and the various places I lived and the
people who shaped me. Maybe I had to honor them in this
way because they are still so much a part of me. Maybe I've
been ducking and dodging "attachments" for years because I
didn't want them to end. Maybe I wasn't supposed to have
closure in the traditional sense, or maybe on the flipside noth-

ing really "ended" and instead everything evolved. Or maybe Mikey's entire existence was a lesson in itself.

I like to think of Mikey moving on after me, rather than simply vanishing or ceasing to exist. Maybe he found a new kid to inspire and help with the seesaw of childhood. Maybe he moved to Imaginary Hills—a place we joked all the imaginary friends moved to after they left their imaginer. Maybe he partied every night with cowboys, dinosaurs, talking cars, and other imaginary friends. Or maybe he's stayed with me, right beside me this whole time, and I never knew.

BACK WHEN WE LIVED ON BERGSTROM AIR FORCE BASE IN AUS-tin, I always dreamed of what my future would look like. I just wanted to know where I was going. What I'd be doing and if everything was going to be all right. I didn't want to live in the future per se, I just wanted to make sure it was as "cool" as Mikey and I thought it would be.

Marty McFly and the Back to the Future franchise gave me a glimpse of *how* I could see the future. And after Mikey and I watched *Back to the Future Part II* for the twenty-third time, I decided I needed to take our future into our own hands. So we set out to build our own time machine using everything we learned from Marty and Doc Brown. First we needed a ride. We needed a DeLorean.

Base housing on Bergstrom Air Force Base primarily con-sisted of structures that were split into single-family homes, duplexes, and triplexes. Behind the long rows of duplexes were rows of covered carports with a shed for storage in the back of each one. Most folks who lived on base didn't use their carport because there was always plenty of street parking, and also Uncle Sam was not paying enlisteds enough to be two-car households. Almost everyone on base did use the storage shed in the back of their carport, though. And those sheds, for my imagination, were filled with gold.

Knowing exactly what we needed to do to get to the future, Mikey and I set out to find all the elements we needed to build our DeLorean. I grabbed my parents' *Encyclopaedia Britannica* from 1969 and researched a car engine—why we owned encyclopedias that were almost as old as my parents, I don't know, but real ones know that's how you found information back in the day. Once Mikey and I knew the parts we were looking for, from a 1969 version of a combustion engine, we set out to find them.

We spent days diving in dumpsters, rummaging through my dad's toolboxes, and thoroughly searching any unlocked storage sheds. In shed after shed, we found tiny things we thought we'd be able to use. And then, finally, we found it. After about five or six mediocre-to-disappointing sheds, we pulled the double doors of shed 1108 open and a fully built engine block was floating in front of us.

"This is it!" I said as we stepped into the room. Mikey nodded his head up and down, "This *is* it." Just outside the shed sat a 1982 fire-engine red IROC Z28 Camaro. The tires were deflated, the top was covered in gray tape, the side-view mirrors had cobwebs all over them, and the IROC Z28 letters had peeled so the logo read I O   28. The Camaro had seen better days, but it was the key to the future.

"We need a flux capacitor," I barked while we gawked at the engine. There was no way this was going to work unless

we had one. And since our days of shed-to-dumpster searching hadn't turned up much in the way of parts, there was
really only one way to expedite the process.

"I know what we need to do." A Cheshire cat grin spread
across Mikey's face, his eyes open like a Vegas poker chip.
"We need to go door-to-door and ask everybody if they have
one," he said.

I knew he was right. The fastest way for me to get to the
future was to go door-to-door telling people what we needed.
I quickly realized that "we" wouldn't be able to do that, because no one, other than my mom, had ever acknowledged
Mikey.

"I'll do it," I said. "You stay here and start mechanic-ing
the engine with the screw-thing and the hammer and I'll go
get us a flux capacitor." Mikey and I did our quick secret
handshake—*slap—slap—dap—turn left—turn right—tickle the
palm—blow it up like a bomb*—and with him inside the shed to
work, I shut the doors and went on my way. "Outtie 5000."

After fourteen minutes of what I considered focused wandering, I tapped my dusty adolescent knuckles across an off-
white hollow-core door. A white guy, buzz cut, probably in
his late twenties, answered the door.

"Nah, I'm not buying candy bars today," he said when he
saw me. In the past I had been through the neighborhood
selling World's Finest Chocolate bars for various causes: karate, the Boy Scouts, and church youth service—but not
today.

"I'm not selling candy!" I blurted before he could shut the
door on me. His face turned quizzical.

"So, what's up?" he asked. I took a deep breath and looked
him in the eye like a prophet starting a cult.

"I'm going to the future to see what it's like and like how cool my life turns out and stuff and to do it I'm going to build a time machine, but first I need a flux capacitor. So, I was wondering if you had one I could borrow? I swear I'll give it back . . . when I get back from the future."

Buzz Cut's quizzical look slowly changed. The corners of his mouth turned up, his eyes opened wider, and his cheeks started to turn red.

"Ahahaha . . . you're gonna . . . ahahaha . . . do what now?" He laughed his way through. I didn't understand what was funny. This was serious. My future depended on it. So, I looked at him and said it again.

"I'm going to the future to see what it's like and like how cool my life turns out and stuff and to do it I'm going to build a time machine, but first I need a flux capacitor. So, I was wondering if you had one I could borrow?"

In a matter of seconds, he went from a laugh-out-loud wide-open cackle to a tight-lipped smile as he tried to explain to me that no one has a flux capacitor because they don't exist. My eyebrows started to furrow as my eyes laser-focused on what I perceived to be his condescending smile.

"Because you don't believe doesn't mean I can't go!" I said through gritted teeth to him, and I stomped away. On to the next.

Eight houses and forty-five minutes later, I was still empty-handed, and the sun was starting to go down. The one rule every kid, regardless of geographic location, knows better than to break is "Be home before the streetlight comes on." With daylight winding down and the potential for an ass-whooping rising, I made my way back to the shed where Mikey was working. When I got there, he was wearing overalls and a headband with a flashlight on it. He was staring at the engine, scratching at his head.

"I think I'm gonna have to take this apart and put it back together. I need to go step-by-step, can't rush it," he said. Then he turned to me, light in my face like an interrogation. "Did you get it?"

Shame washed over me. My shoulders rolled forward. My eyes shot down to the floor. I shook my head no. Mikey placed his hand on my slumped shoulders. "It's all good. We'll get it tomorrow. Somebody around here has to have one. I mean, we're on a military base."

I looked up, feeling relieved.

"I'm gonna stay here and work on this tonight so we're ready to go after school tomorrow," he said.

My face scrunched up. "You gonna stay out here? All night?"

Mikey nodded. "Yeah. I'll work on this. It's going to take some time but it'll get there."

Before I left, Mikey looked out the doors and noticed the dusk sky, and said, "You'll be good. You got this."

THE NEXT MORNING, MIKEY WASN'T THERE WHEN I WOKE UP, HE didn't ride the bus to school with me, and his spot at the cafeteria table sat empty. I went an entire school day without seeing Mikey. That was the first time that had happened since we met. And from then on, even though I didn't realize it at the time, my in-person run-ins with Mikey began to become less frequent. Sometimes it'd be a few hours. Sometimes it'd be a full day.

As I grew older, Mikey moved farther and farther into my

rearview. First an unrecognizable face, then a figure deep in the distance, and ultimately a speck that disappeared into the air. At the same time, I became more aware of the world. I lost my innocence to the societal pressures of "living in the real world" and "being a man."

I never thought about what my future would be like without Mikey. Since I had known him, he was the one consistent presence in my life, other than my parents, to whom I never had to say goodbye. For all the futuristic time-traveling DeLoreans we'd drive, the balling-out-of-control-in-fur-coats-while-carrying-bags-full-of-tokens strides through arcades we had, and the best-friend-forever dreams we shared, I never imagined my future without him. It never crossed ~~our~~ my mind. I never thought that Mikey and I wouldn't be in each other's lives.

Maybe that's because we still are.

For the record, I am fully aware, and have been for a very, very long time now, that Mikey was a figment of my childhood imagination. But even with that realization and having the perspective of looking back, Mikey is still as much a part of my childhood as seeing *Boyz N the Hood* for the first time, dodging my first kiss with West Covina, and taking hella long road trips in the Previa with my grandparents. My childhood in a lot of ways was shaped by his presence, and my entire adult life has been shaped by my childhood.

As I pushed through my late teens, the voice in my head started becoming the voice formerly known as Mikey. It became my subconscious.

After Mikey left, the voice I thought belonged to him and

that was helping me navigate my childhood was, of course, my own voice and way of coping and processing things I couldn't talk to a sibling, parent, or anyone else about. As I got older, that voice didn't "leave"; in fact, it had its work cut out. I still needed a lot of hyping-up to do the things I was afraid or anxious to do. Like the time I played full-court one-on-one as a freshman in high school with Ryan "Skywalker" Humphrey back at Booker T. From the outset, I was out of my league. It was a real-life representation of Kadir Nelson's *David and Goliath* lithograph. Playing against "Hump," I needed the voice in my head that day when he literally flew through the air like Superman and dunked on me . . . repeatedly! I scored on him a few times, though. Hit him with a one-two he didn't see coming, and he stumbled back. One might say, "I got them anklessssss!"

ALL THOSE YEARS RUNNING AROUND WITH MIKEY, ALL THOSE years with Mikey as a voice in my head and then the subsequent years listening to my subconscious, I came to realize Mikey/my subconscious was preparing me for life. Teaching me how to think for myself, inspire myself, protect what's sacred, and how to survive.

Because Mikey was like my flux capacitor. He was the catalyst that made me believe, imagine, and grow. Having Mikey in my life allowed me the benefit of simulating what I thought at the time were profoundly complex social situations. I had adventures with Mikey that I didn't have to share with anyone else; I could hold them close to me. I believe that at a very young age there was a convergence: My subconscious was realizing the world around me was far out of my control, and yet in the chaos of the '90s and my moving around every few years, all I wanted to do was find something, anything, that I, as a stubborn Capricorn only child, could actually control. Mikey was my way of taking control, a coping mechanism, for such a confusing time.

I understand that Mikey's feelings were my feelings—I've known that for a long time—however, as a child, separating the two helped me understand emotions and cope with them. Mikey was my imagination's way of trying to make sense of the Rorschach-like confusing world we lived in. He was a fully realized person for me—there to be scared with me, talk me out of bad decisions, hype me up when I was down, and make me think anything was possible. Mikey was essential for my survival back then because with every move to a new school, every summer in Sac, and every new set of social interactions, I learned a new lesson that prepared me for my future of navigating teenage life and even early adulthood. But most importantly, I got to play.

With Mikey long gone and me being lucky enough to live my dream of playing make-believe every day for my day job, reflecting back on my childhood has made me realize that whether we know it or not, we all have a voice that guides us and helps us become the person we are today . . . for good or bad! It's a radical act to choose joy, adventure, curiosity, play, and freedom. And sometimes, if you listen close enough to that voice and allow yourself just a few minutes to tune out all the adult stuff that our very serious and very busy lives are throwing at us, that voice is our sense of play, our sense of joy, and our sense of imagination saying, "Let me back in!!!"

ACKNOWLEDGMENTS

SOMEWHERE IN MY HEAD

Thank you!

There are a lot of people who made this book possible, even though many of them may never know it: My great-grandparents and grandparents, maternal and paternal, for taking me in every summer, letting me stay up late every night, and taking me on the longest, hottest road trips. My aunts and uncles for "not stuttin' me," facilitating consistent family functions, never-ending prayers, and education in "cool." My cousins for running around with me, running after me, and running away from me. Teammates and coaches who endured my turnovers, obtuse shot selection, and hoop dreams of grandeur. The KRU 2 Live to ever forget—Marshall, Will, Jesse, Jason, Joe, Juan, Joseph, and Vernon—for every party, every pickup game, every argument, every Braum's burger and Taco Bueno burrito, every Sunday afternoon listening to Playa 1000. Every city that raised me and let me raise hell. My mom for bringing me into the world, and my dad for not taking me out of it all those times I got in trouble. And for nurturing my imagination and pushing me to dream. Thank you!

AB, you read the very first paragraph I wrote on this. Thank you for your notes, at least the good ones. Thank you to the mad wizard–like brain of Albert Lee for understanding this crazy idea I had and pushing me to do it. Thank you, Nicole Counts, for listening to my long boundless voice-notes, reading my long typo-filled emails, and teaching me how to do this even when I questioned: *Why am I doing this?* You're a living legend. I'm forever grateful. To Donovan X. Ramsey for being brilliant, Safia Elhillo for being unwavering, and Fatimah Asghar for being motivational in times when I wanted to quit—y'all provided a safe space and community. Thank you!

To my wife for listening to me talk about this book for days that added to weeks that added to months that added to years, and constantly making the space I needed to write it. And to my daughter for stepping on my computer, erasing two chapters, and never giving up on your loving mission to love me but not let me write in peace. Thank you!

ABOUT THE AUTHOR

Born in Sumter, South Carolina, to a military family, JAY ELLIS spent his childhood ducking and dodging his cousins while inventing new personas for every town he landed in. Too many to count. After college, he realized the NBA wasn't good enough for him and he didn't want to crush other players' dreams as he dominated the league, so he decided to take his one-man show to Hollywood, where he got his start on BET's *The Game*. Now an accomplished actor, philanthropist, and entrepreneur, Jay is best known for his role as the boyfriend you love to hate but you really love, Lawrence on HBO's *Insecure*, for which he won an NAACP Image Award. He appeared alongside Tom Cruise flying jets through the skies in the Oscar-nominated film *Top Gun: Maverick*. When he's not on set filming he spends the majority of his days cleaning up the messes that his daughter's imaginary friend "Jack" made. Karma.

ABOUT THE TYPE

This book was set in Dante, a typeface designed by Giovanni Mardersteig (1892–1977). Conceived as a private type for the Officina Bodoni in Verona, Italy, Dante was originally cut only for hand composition by Charles Malin, the famous Parisian punch cutter, between 1946 and 1952. Its first use was in an edition of Boccaccio's *Trattatello in laude di Dante* that appeared in 1954. The Monotype Corporation's version of Dante followed in 1957. Though modeled on the Aldine type used for Pietro Cardinal Bembo's treatise *De Aetna* in 1495, Dante is a thoroughly modern interpretation of that venerable face.